Praise for
Liars, Cheats, and Creeps

I am inspired by these four courageous survivors of abuse who found their voices and regained control of their lives. Their stories provide a rare glimpse into the recovery process for women who endure and survive domestic abuse. My work as an advocate for survivors is reaffirmed by their bravery and resilience.

> –Laura Kovach, M.Ed., Director of Women's Center at Georgetown University, Faculty in Women's and Gender Studies Program, Georgetown University, Washington, D.C.

This powerful book sheds light on the dark truths some people would like to keep hidden. Dr. Martin brought these women together and inspired courage to overcome the darkness within their lives. So many people need to hear their powerful stories, including those who are suffering, loved ones, and professionals.

—Dr. Lina Racicot, Director of Graduate Psychology, American International College, Springfield, MA.

Poignant, witty, and life affirming are the three words I use to identify these four strong women. Life may have thrown horrific curves their way, but together they learned lessons from which we can all benefit. Thank you!

—C. Lee Bennett, Captain, Retired, Springfield Police Department, Domestic Violence Unit, Springfield, MA., Adjunct faculty at Westfield State University, Westfield, MA. and Bay Path University, Longmeadow, MA.

Liars, Cheats, and Creeps provides valuable insight into the benefits of group therapy for anyone who faces the challenge of a high conflict divorce with a history of an abusive relationship. Dr. Martin offers sensible, practical tools to help parents reduce conflict and survive with a new outlook, which in turn protects the well-being of their children. Women who fear divorce will find support and guidance from the members of this therapy group.

> –Attorney Mary A. Samberg, Parenting Coordinator and Guardian Ad Litem, West Springfield, MA.

AMAZING is the only word to describe these stories of four remarkable women and their journey as members of a support group. For a year they leaned on each other in an effort to put their lives on track after domestic abuse. Through the victims' stories, the authors instruct on domestic abuse, discuss what to consider, and show how to break free of abusive relationships. An empowering presentation!

> Mary A. Socha, J.D. Family Court Attorney, West Springfield, MA., Board Member, Woman Shelter Compañeras, Holyoke, MA

This inspiring book invites us to join group therapy sessions, and embrace the stories without judging, as four troubled women seek answers and let go of self-blaming. Dr. Martin addresses the topics of power, control, deceit, and betrayal. These are things millions of women deal with every day but are afraid and/or embarrassed to talk about.

> –Milta Vargas, Domestic Violence Coordinator, Springfield Police Department, Springfield, MA.

Books by Patricia Peters Martin, Ph.D. and Renee Forte

Liars, Cheats, and Creeps:
Leaving the Narcissist Behind

Moving on from a Narcissist

Books by Patricia Peters Martin, Ph.D. and Helene De Montreux Houston, MS. APRN

The Patient Knows: Wisdom from
THE OTHER COUCH

Age Well:
8 Dimensions of Wellness as You Age

Incudes new information on
HEALING AND POST-TRAUMATIC GROWTH

MOVING ON FROM A NARCISSIST

*How four women found happiness
after leaving
liars, cheats, and creeps*

PATRICIA PETERS MARTIN, Ph. D.
RENEE FORTE

Moving on from a Narcissist: How Four Women Found Happiness after Leaving Liars, Cheats, and Creeps

ISBN: 979-8-9989139-0-7

Copyright © 2023, 2025 by Patricia Peters Martin, Ph.D. and Renee Forte

All rights reserved. No part of this book may be reproduced or transmitted in any form or by any means, electronic or mechanical, including photocopying, recording, or by any information storage and retrieval system, without written permission from the authors, except for the inclusion of brief quotations in a review.

First printing, 2023, as Moving on from a Narcissistic Sociopath: How Four Women Found Happiness after Leaving Liars, Cheats, and Creeps

Second printing, 2025

PetersMartinPress
38 Oxford Road
Longmeadow, MA 01106

Dedication

We dedicate this book to all who have struggled in abusive relationships and found the courage to leave the darkness and seek recovery. For those who continue living with violence, may this book help you find your way to healing.

Contents

Introduction..11

PART I: The Group 21

    Members of The Group 21

    Who Are These Men?.. 26

    How Do Smart Women get involved
    with abusive men? 29

    Why did the men choose these
    women to marry and have children? 31

    Getting Out 33

PART II: The Reunion 36

    Contact With the Ex 40

    Children and Finances... 53

    Dating or Not Dating... 82

    Creating the House of Love................................... 103

    Looking Back 107

    Discussion of Healing.. 128

    Looking Forward...148

PART III: Things You Need to Know 152

Safety Advice 156

Recovery Toolkit 160

Types of Therapy 175

Post-Traumatic Growth: Envision
Your Future in Five Years 177

Your Five-Year Plan 179

In Closing 184

RESOURCES 186

APPS for PC and Devices 189

BOOKS and ARTICLES: 190

HOTLINES: 192

About the Authors 194

INTRODUCTION

This book is written as a lifeline for women involved with men who lie, cheat, and otherwise mistreat them.

In my busy practice as a clinical psychologist, I often helped clients who were hurt, angry, and astonished by betrayal from men they trusted. Their husbands' behavior appeared to have a pattern—and most of my clients were surprised to learn the toxic behaviors they lived with were a chilling combination of two personality disorders.

Narcissistic sociopath is the clinical diagnosis for these men, and you'll learn more about them in this book. As part of this deep-seated personality disorder, such people are often charming, manipulative, addicted, potentially violent, and difficult to escape from.

When you're involved with a liar, cheat, or creep, nothing is simple or straightforward. Separating and divorcing such people brings emotional turmoil, pain, frustration, doubt, and even fear for your safety. As this book will attest, healing and moving beyond the abuser's control takes time and patience. Moving on with your life is a huge challenge when you're involved with someone who exploits and disposes of other people.

I am a licensed doctoral level clinical psychologist and my coauthor, Renee Forte, is an intimate partner abuse survivor who chooses not to reveal her real name.

The book also features the voices and wisdom of four brave women who survived intimate partner violence.

Almost every divorce is a wrenching experience. The aftermath is also difficult, but time and counseling go a long way to heal ex-partners so they can move on to lead healthy, productive lives.

However, many women discover that divorces involving betrayal, infidelity, alcoholism, drug abuse, and sometimes physical violence are especially difficult. In these cases, spouses are hurt and angry, and the legal procedure is extra stressful.

Then there are high conflict divorces involving narcissistic sociopaths. This type of intimate partner abuse involves emotional, psychological, and often physical violence. Divorces are not only grueling for the spouse who wants out, but are also hard on attorneys and the judges involved.

The abusers are expert con artists who manipulate the legal process in any way possible. Their goal is to continue punishing and causing pain before, during, and after the divorce.

With this in mind, Renee and I coauthored the book *Liars, Cheats and Creeps: Leaving the Narcissist Behind*[1] (referred to here as LCC 1). Our book focused on the relationships of male abusers to female partners because this is the most prevalent type of abuse. However, abuse occurs in homosexual relationships as well, and from women to men in heterosexual relationships. The advice in this book is applicable to all variations of partner abuse.

Renee and I are writing this new book to let women know they face a long road to recovery after leaving a narcissistic sociopath. We want to help you get through this difficult time in your life. You have been through the wringer! We most definitely do *not* want to dissuade you from getting away and staying away from your abuser. Rather, we hope this book will encourage you to *get going* on the road to good health and well-being, even though the journey may be an arduous road trip.

[1] Martin, Patricia, and Forte, Renee. Liars, Cheats and Creeps: Leaving the Narcissist Behind. Longmeadow, MA: PetersMartinPress, 2025

If you're reading this book while still in an abusive relationship, we advise you to seek counseling if at all possible. You can also read *Liars, Cheats, and Creeps: Leaving the Narcissist Behind* to help you feel as though you belong to a supportive group of women who've been through what you're now experiencing.

You should also consult our resources listed online and in Part 3 of this book. In addition, your local women's shelter may offer a wealth of information and resources. Please know you are not alone. You are not stupid for being in a dreadful relationship. You need and deserve support.

The Liars, Cheats, and Creeps Support Group

The four women who joined our support group years ago met to share their experiences and help each other. Their lives were falling apart. They entered individual therapy broken, desperate and not knowing which way to turn. They were anxious and generally shed rivers of tears the first time they met with me.

Each of them felt lost and knew they needed help. After counseling each of the women for several months, I organized The Group to show each of these women, who felt trapped and alone in destructive and complicated marriages, that they were not alone. Not by a long shot. We all found care and strength in The Group. The 52 sessions in the book, LCC 1, are meant to be the next best thing to joining a live support group.

The four women learned about the narcissistic and sociopathic personality types to whom they were married. They began to understand how power and control were the driving forces behind much of their husbands' behavior. The terms gaslighting and covert emotional and psychological abuse were all discussed in the first book. The Group also came to understand why they married these liars, cheats, and creeps. Ultimately these four women in The Group supported each other in leaving their abusive marriages.

If you left an abusive relationship, we say "Congratulations, you got out!"

If you're in the process of separation—keep going! It takes courage and perseverance to escape the clutches of an abuser, and you'll need continued bravery as you face the challenges ahead. But, remember—you did it. You got away! Divorcing a narcissist is hell, but staying with a narcissist is a greater hell!

Only by leaving an abusive relationship can you claim and rebuild your true self. Winston Churchill, prime minister of Great Britain during World War II, said: "If you're going through hell, keep going!"

You may feel your life is a battlefield, but keep going!

You may feel the divorce process is never-ending, but keep going!

You may sometimes feel alone and desperate, but don't give up. There is light at the end of this dark tunnel, and you will restore peace and sanity to your life.

In these pages, the four brave women of The Group want to share their experiences after divorce to help you understand what may lie ahead on your road to recovery.

Like these women, perhaps you believed when you finally separated and divorced, the abusive behavior was in your rear-view mirror. But the reality is, although you divorce the abuser and you're working to become an independent woman controlling her own destiny, **your abuser has not changed.** He will remain the same, angry, entitled person motivated by wanting control and power over you.

You may continue to be his target, but remember, *you are not the same person.* You see things differently now and you're becoming stronger and more aware.

The wise women in The Group are survivors who want to assure you that leaving the abuser is absolutely worth it! Being prepared for the hazards on the road ahead and knowing you are not alone not only frees you; it is empowering.

The Effects of Abuse

We will talk about the long-term effects of abuse and how you can rebuild a healthy and fulfilling life for yourself and your family. By exploring the lives of the women in The Group, you'll see what difficulties lie ahead, and how to navigate these hazards as you reclaim control of your life.

Each woman in The Group wants to share her journey so you'll be forewarned about the problems she encountered. As you absorb the voices of women in The Group and my guidance as a therapist, we want you to know you are not stupid, not worthless, and most definitely not alone on this road.

First, a disclaimer. As with LCC 1, we did not record individual interviews or reunion meetings of The Group. The sessions were in utmost privacy. Conversations are reconstructed from our memory—which is pretty darn good. As in LCC 1, details have been changed to protect the identities of the women and their children and safeguard them from their abusers. However, the experiences and feelings recounted are all too real.

This poem by Barbara Ardinger expresses the value of sisterhood and is used with her permission.

There is a Web of Women.

There is a web of women
living lightly in the world
As gently as hand upon forehead, checking for fever,
the web touches the pulse of the planet with intention
to help
to heal
to comfort.
There is a flood of women weeping softly for the world.
As tender as hand upon heart, cherishing her precious children,
The web cries for lost intention
to heal
to comfort
to help.
There is a circle of women dancing joyfully through the world.
As exultant as hand touching yoni, celebrating our mysteries,
the web sings for intention found again
to comfort
to help
to heal.
There is a web of women tenderly enclosing the world.
As sturdy as hands setting roots, planting community,
the web encircles intention held
to help
to heal
to comfort.

This book is divided into three parts:

Part 1 sets the stage and describes members of The Group and the toxic nature of their marriages. How did they get into the relationships? Why did they stay? How did they get out? Who are these men?

Part 2 is where members of The Group share their experiences after divorce, including how they detached and set boundaries, navigated issues with children and finances, decided to date or not, and finally embarked on healing self-journeys. I will be advising throughout the book.

Part 3 contains resources and guidance to help you navigate the post-divorce journey. We will provide safety tips and healing steps to create a healthy, empowered, and sane new you.

Patricia Martin, Ph.D.

Renee Forte

PART I: THE GROUP

Members of The Group

Dr. Pat: Some of the most depleted and desperate clients in my practice are women who married narcissistic sociopaths. I use the term sociopath to describe the current diagnosis of Antisocial Personality Disorder in the DSM V.[2] The term Sociopathic Personality Disorder from the DSM IV more accurately describes the type of men we refer to in this book. Personally, as a doctoral level clinical psychologist, I believe the Antisocial Personality label is far too euphemistic and whitewashes the type of people who fit this diagnosis. Therefore, throughout this book, we will use "narcissistic sociopath" to label the men about whom we speak.

The women in The Group all felt broken, alone, frightened and bewildered when their marital dreams turned

---

[2] *The Diagnostic and Statistical Manual of Mental Disorders*, Fifth Edition, (DSM-5). This is a resource to help healthcare providers diagnose mental disorders.

into nightmares. Each of them sought individual counseling with me to try and make sense of what was happening in their lives, to understand these men, and to ask if they were going crazy. They all felt confused, frightened, and anxious. Depression and despair set in, and they needed help.

After many sessions of individual therapy, I asked four of my clients, all mothers and contributing members of their communities, if they'd like to get together with other women who were divorcing husbands with similar issues. My suggestion met with a unanimous YES! and they met as a group over ten years to share and support one another.

Now, years have passed since the four members of The Group last saw one another. Renee and I contacted each of them to see how they were doing and ask if they'd like to meet again and help other women by sharing their experiences after divorce. Each one eagerly agreed. Stephanie, Sharon, Debbie and Renee have been separated or divorced for almost ten or more years, and they have a lot to share.

First, let us take you back in time and introduce the women when they first met as The Group:

Stephanie: 46 years old. Married 19 years. She was on the verge of divorce at the start of The Group. Her two sons were teenagers at the time and she worked in a grocery store, although she had a college degree in Sociology. Years before, she was active at her sons' school, and volunteered at the local library. As her marriage worsened, she became more isolated. Her husband drank too much and was increasingly controlling, abusive and violent. He shoved her and choked her. In one incident, he threw a toaster at her. After separation, he kicked in her back door—enraged, yelling horrible insults and threats. He was arrested twice. Even the neighbors were worried for Stephanie.

Sharon: 42 years old. Married nine years. At the time The Group first met, Sharon had two children: a son who was seven and a daughter five years old. She has a journalism degree from NYU and moved to our area after marriage. Sharon was a stay-at-home mom. Her husband was an executive in a pharmaceutical company who often traveled, and her only peace came while he was away. He'd become increasingly abusive. He shoved her against the wall in their garage, pushed her out of a moving car, and threw her out of the house in the winter and locked the door to teach her a lesson. He told her she was a terrible wife and mother. Her mom helped her when possible. Sharon was frightened of her husband.

Debbie: 57 years old. Married for 24 years. Divorced two years before The Group. Debbie had two daughters who were 20 and 17 years old. Before marriage she worked in the hospitality business for a hotel chain. She loved travel and was the primary bread winner. After marriage, she worked part time when her kids were small. She and her husband bought a restaurant together and his job was to manage that business. He drank a lot, but seemed to stop when she gave him an ultimatum. After a while he became more and more absent from the family. She hired a private investigator who reported on her husband's affair with a woman. She called her Ex "Cheater" until the end of LCC 1, when she started feeling sorry for him. Debbie crafts jewelry as a hobby. She was active in her church.

Renee: 59 years old. Married for 28 years. She had divorced two years before The Group began meeting, but was still unsteady. Her four children ranged in age from 21 to 29. Renee worked as a tax preparer for a large firm before marriage, and then worked part time from home when the kids were young. Things blew up when her husband, Bob, an accountant, came home from work one night to tell her she should be tested for gonorrhea. She tested positive, underwent treatment, and had to be tested several times for HIV. She soon learned her husband bought women throughout their long marriage. He admitted he was *never* faithful. He would tell the family he had to work all the time "for the family." After these explosive revelations, Renee felt like "road kill" and considered suicide to stop the pain of his betrayal. Thankfully, she stayed alive for her children. She once loved to cook and garden, but her ex whittled away at her self-esteem. He was critical and demeaning towards her throughout their marriage, although not physically abusive. Nevertheless, Renee was emotionally and psychologically bruised and almost broken.

Who Are These Men?

I first suggested meeting as a group because these women had something in common: they each had husbands who abused them emotionally, psychologically, financially, and some physically. These men all fit into the categories of narcissism, sociopathy, pathological liar, and bully. In short, these partners were liars, cheats and creeps who abused their wives while married and through the divorce process—and still caused disruptions one, five and even ten years after divorce. The women changed. Their ex-husbands did not.

The primary characteristics of people with **narcissistic personality disorder** include an inflated sense of self-importance, a deep need for admiration, and lack of empathy for others.

Behind their mask of ultra-confidence lies a fragile self-esteem that's vulnerable to the slightest criticism. Living with a narcissistic person is difficult because they become angry and impatient when they don't receive special treatment. Narcissists come across as conceited, boastful, and pretentious. They tend to monopolize conversations and look down on others as inferior to them. Narcissists have trouble handling anything that may be perceived as criticism; they react with rage and contempt and try to belittle other people to make themselves feel superior.

A **sociopath** is more dangerous than a narcissist because these people have no regard for right and wrong and often disregard the rights, wishes, and feelings of others. They lack a conscience.

The symptoms of a narcissist and sociopath often overlap, but someone with a sociopathic personality disorder has no awareness of, or regard for, other people's feelings. They have no remorse for their hurtful actions. They are often adept and accurate in perceiving how other people think, but with no real understanding or regard for feelings. They are master manipulators.

Men are at greater risk for sociopathic personality disorder. The Diagnostic and Statistical Manual of Psychological Diagnoses says sociopaths are 3% of the male population and 1% of the female population.

If you're living with a sociopath, you're likely to see the following:

- verbal and physical abuse,
- frequent lying,
- reckless behavior,
- risky sexual behavior,
- con artist behavior and lying to others,
- feeling no remorse and justifying their behavior after harming others.
- They often steal, vandalize, are violent, show cruelty to animals, and are bullying and violent toward people in their lives.

Sociopaths will harm those closest to them through psychological, physical and emotional abuse, control of finances, and by sexual exploitation.

After discussing these traits, The Group created the title for *Liars, Cheats and Creeps: Leaving the Narcissist Behind*. The phrase "liars, cheats and creeps" is a colloquial way of describing the narcissistic and sociopathic personality disorders.

How Do Smart Women get involved with abusive men?

In a word: Charm. The outward persona of a narcissistic sociopath is an interesting, exciting, unpredictable, and charming person. Sharon recalls being "swept off her feet" by a dashing executive who showered her with attention, gifts, and promises of a wonderful life.

Stephanie recalls the man she fell in love with as being fun loving and the life of the party. Renee and Debbie were smitten by the wit and intelligence of the men they eventually married. There was romance. There were good times and promises of commitment, fidelity and raising children together.

Problems soon developed. Periodic criticism grew to constant belittling. Suspicions grew into surveillance. Substance abuse increased in frequency. There were frequent absences. The husbands grew short tempered, mocking, and disrespectful. There was escalating criticism over money, housekeeping, appearance, friends, and family. The women were blamed for every big and little thing. There was rough sex or no sex. For some women, insults turned into physical violence.

At the beginning of therapy and The Group, each member was in coping mode. They felt confused. After all—they fell in love with these men, had children with them, and wanted more than anything for their husbands to go back to being the wonderful men they first met. These loyal women "hung in there," trying to make themselves attractive, their children well behaved, and their houses meticulously clean. By shrinking their own needs and wants, they hoped to lessen the stresses on their husbands. In their minds, stress had to explain and even excuse their husbands' attitude changes and abusive behavior.

But they didn't label the abuse at first. They thought it was their challenge in the marriage to deal with a high strung or eccentric and powerful man.

This is called "enabling." And it's understandable. After all, the guys were charming; they promised love and support. The women thought they should be smart enough to figure out how to make things work for their husbands. They told themselves, "Just try this and try that. Strive for perfection and all will be well. Keep the family intact no matter the cost."

Droplets of periodic affection fueled false hope. And there were children to consider. So, the women stayed even as the abuse grew, usually in proportion to their attempts at placating their husbands.

There are many reasons to stay in an unhappy marriage: religious reasons, financial dependency, isolation, family pressure, protecting their children, and just hoping things will get better.

These women had an additional reason: Fear. They made excuses for their husbands' behavior and excuses for themselves to stay. Fear of their husbands' wrath left them paralyzed into inaction for far too long, and blocked their thinking about how to get out and live saner lives.

Why did the men choose these women to marry and have children?

The women in The Group were smart, accomplished, interesting, charming and attractive. They were also very trusting. Looking back to when they were dating, the members realized they overlooked red flags. But who sees red flags when you're falling in love? They were victims of expert con men who hid their true selves until they couldn't or wouldn't any more. Wives were like stage props in their selfish minds. They wanted someone to love them, take care of them, obey, and admire them. They wanted children because that was the script they were following. Outward appearance was everything to them.

Whatever love they ever felt for their wives and children, it was far less than their self-love and inflated egos.

Often women who marry sociopathic narcissists have had limited dating experience. Many of these women were from families where fathers treated their wives kindly, so the women anticipated the same from their husbands. Many women in these relationships are also highly empathetic, with so much empathy they'd worry more about how the people around them felt rather than how they themself were doing emotionally. When a charming, manipulative con man came along, they were hooked.

Getting Out

Each woman finally experienced a cataclysmic event or last straw. Perhaps it was being screamed at yet again because dinner wasn't perfect, the children hadn't picked up their toys, a shirt was ruined in the laundry, or a bill was too high. It could have been a black eye, getting choked, or marital rape. Somehow, a desperate call for help to family, friends or a hotline led to finding a way out.

Seeking help takes enormous courage. First, you must admit you cannot fix the problems. You must be willing to stop minimizing and excusing the episodes of yelling and psychological or physical violence, and see what others around you may have already seen.

Counseling gave these women a reality check that their relationships were unhealthy and no amount of wishing, trying, and praying would make any lasting improvements. Counseling also "flipped the script" that the divorce option is not a failure, but rather the best way out. They had to learn that staying in an abusive marriage was harming themselves and their children. They had to learn that keeping the family intact at all costs was a false goal, because they were already a dysfunctional family.

After the tough decision to divorce came safety planning, attorneys, and many legal forms to fill out.

Meeting with The Group showed each of the women they were not alone or stupid. They were vulnerable and trusting. They believed lies. They were conned by experts at manipulation and, unfortunately, their divorces would be long and contentious.

Dr. Pat's Notes on Getting Out

- You may experience a cataclysmic event or last straw that drives you to seek help and take action.
- You must admit you cannot fix the problems. Stop minimizing and excusing your abuser's behavior. You've been abused by a charming, manipulative con man who only cares about his own needs.
- Seeking help takes courage, but divorce is not a failure – it's your pathway to a better life.
- Seeking help takes determination, but you can do this!

You can't go back and change the beginning. But you can start where you are and change the ending. –C.S. Lewis

PART II:
THE REUNION

The group met in Dr. Pat's office for their reunion. Little had changed there since the last meeting: Same couch and chairs. Maybe even the same pillows!

As the women arrived, they exchanged hugs and everyone started talking at once.

Dr. Pat: Welcome all! So good to see you! Please sit down so we can get started. Thank you for coming to share your experiences. I know it isn't easy to look back at such a painful part of your lives. I see you all as wise women and true survivors who are busy and leading full lives. You are generous in being here tonight to share your stories so other women can learn from you about the hazards they should expect after divorcing a narcissistic sociopath.

You're even sitting where you usually sat! I'll try to keep our conversation moving along and focused on selecting the topics we'll discuss. Let's start by having each of you describe your divorce in a word or sentence.

Debbie: Divorce was an ordeal and a trial by fire. I got burned a lot, but I survived.

Stephanie: It was a dumpster fire!

Renee: It was like an earthquake from the time he told me he caught gonorrhea from a woman he prostituted, all the way to the final divorce decree. My divorce took over three years. It was expensive and exhausting because he fought me over everything.

Sharon: I tried to turn off my emotions and plow through it. But it was like walking through a minefield with things blowing up at each step. I don't know how I got through it, but I saved what little energy I had for my kids. I'm so grateful for my counseling sessions with you, Pat, and for the support from The Group.

Dr. Pat: First, let me say I appreciate your kind words about my help, but it's important to recognize that each of you was essential to the healing. You—The Group—fed and nurtured one another. I was simply a guide.

Regarding your divorces, I understand exactly why you compare it to a dumpster fire, a minefield, an earthquake, and trial by fire. Those are perfect words to describe what many women experience when they divorce a controlling, abusive man.

But the good news is—you're all here today. Look at each of you now! Getting a divorce was a brave thing. Making this move took courage and, as you found out, the process required a lot of stamina.

Some people view divorce as breaking up a family. But that's not correct. Your families were already broken by the abuse. Divorce is really an act of hope—for yourselves and your children – that your lives can be safer and saner. You all stood up for yourselves to build a better life for yourselves and your children. You should be proud of yourselves. I'm so happy for you!

Sharon: But it feels like I'm still going through the divorce!

Dr. Pat: Yes, I know. That's why we're here tonight, and why Renee and I are writing our second book.

It's common to have a tough time after leaving a narcissistic sociopath. You may leave physically, but the emotional trauma will linger. Plus, your ex is still a devious and vindictive person. Your safety may be at risk, and unless he's moved on to another victim, the abuser will probably try to maintain power and control over you. There may be setbacks, but remember to be kind and patient with yourself.

Never underestimate your abuser's potential for violence, and never let others minimize your perception of risk. According to US Department of Justice, 75% of domestic assaults reported to law enforcement were inflicted after the couples separated. You need to remain vigilant and listen to your gut.

For tonight's session, let's share how much contact you've had, if any, with your "exes." Then we can figure out the topics you want to share and suggestions for future meetings.

Dr. Pat's Notes on the Reunion Meeting

- It's common to have a tough time after leaving a narcissistic sociopath. Be kind and patient with yourself.
- You need to remain vigilant and listen to your instincts.
- Never underestimate your abuser's potential for violence, and never let others minimize your perception of risk.
- Divorce is not breaking up a family. Your abuser already did that. You are finding a better life for yourself and your children.

Contact With the Ex

Dr. Pat: Can each of you describe contact with the ex since your divorce, either by court order or not, and how you felt about it?

Renee: I haven't seen him since the last day in court, over ten years ago. And I didn't even look at him then. I had a final settlement, so no alimony. My children were already adults, so there were no custody issues or child support, except he had to continue paying some college loans for two years.

My settlement includes a permanent protective order and he has adhered to it. Thank you, God! But from time to time, I found weird things on my driveway in front of the house, like once a pile of garbage, and another time a pile of cigarette butts. He smoked and I didn't like that, so I guess that was his calling card.

Another time I found a pile of used condoms. Gross. I also had purple paint thrown at my house and splashed all over the door. All I know is I'm out of a horrible marriage, but he still lives in the area. In fact, he bought a house next door to a close friend. Can you believe it?

I avoid his haunts because I don't want to run into him. At first, my friends would tell me if they saw him somewhere, but I put a stop to that. I told them that info should be on a "need to know basis," if they thought my safety or the safety of any of my kids was at issue. I seldom think of him. I don't have to and I don't want to.

Dr. Pat: Do you know if he remarried?

Renee: I think so. As I said, he bought a house next door to a close friend of mine. She said he's either living with someone or has a wife. I couldn't care less, but I hate that he lives next door to my friend. She comes to visit me at my house, but I never go there anymore.

Dr. Pat: That's too bad, Renee – that he bought a house near your friend. It's an example of him trying to hover over your life, and wanting to remain in your thoughts and fears. The stuff that was dumped on your driveway – it was probably him telling you that you're garbage, and he still smokes and has sex. Big deal. He really is an adolescent, isn't he? But guess what? Purple is a spiritual color that represents power and independence. It's the color used to signify surviving domestic violence.

Renee: I'm sure he didn't know that.

Stephanie: As I always say, karma is a bitch!

Dr. Pat: One great thing about your divorce is not having the ties of alimony or child support. A clean break is great if you can get it. Most women can't. And you may be lucky he has another partner. Narcissistic sociopaths often look for someone else to control right away, so he probably moved on to his next victim. That's good for you, and I'm glad for you that he mostly keeps away.

Debbie: I'm happy for you that he's out of your life, Renee. My story isn't quite as smooth. We have two daughters. I was the primary bread winner, so no alimony payments, but he was supposed to pay some child support. I had custody of the kids because he didn't want them. No custody fight, fortunately. Instead of alimony, I got the house – with the mortgage of course – and he was supposed to buy me out of our restaurant business. That all blew up.

Dr. Pat: Do you have contact with him?

Debbie: He was already living with a woman when we divorced and then he married her right after the divorce became final. His second marriage lasted about a year. His alcoholism caught up with him. He lost everything and he would call me to talk a few times a year. I took his calls and listened. He was lonely. His health suffered because of the drinking, and he's been in and out of hospitals and rehab.

I felt sorry for him. I still do. He used to call and ask for money, but I said no and he doesn't ask any more. One time he sounded bad, so I went over to his crummy apartment to check on him and saw he had no food in the refrigerator. I went to the store and bought him some food. That was it, though. I dropped the groceries off and went home. Was that wrong?

Dr. Pat: There is no right or wrong as long as you're careful about your safety and not becoming entangled again. You had no restraining orders, so you can have contact. Sometimes you can have feelings or pity for your past abuser even ten years later. But you need to remember why you left him in the first place so you don't get sucked back into his dependency and neediness.

Stephanie: When I divorced, I had child support and alimony awarded, but my ex is far in arrears. He owes me big time, like three and a half years' worth. It's expensive to get a lawyer so I let too much time go by, but I'm finally acting now. I have to count every penny. He has a steady job—over 25 years with the same company. My two boys were teenagers when we divorced, and he was supposed to pay child support until each one was 21. He was also to pay for college if they went. I cannot believe I'm still dealing with courts! I have a hearing next month on his arrears, and he has counter-filed asking for alimony to end and for his back alimony to be almost completely reduced.

I don't have any direct contact with him. I have a permanent protective order, which I finally got after he was arrested twice for bashing in my door and throwing a toaster at me. That was my third try at requesting the judge to order him to stay away from me. The first two times I requested a protective order, the judge said divorce is a stressful time for the parties and causes some bad behavior. The third time, I asked the judge if I could speak. I told her the violence and abuse had been going on for many years and was the main reason I sought a divorce and a permanent restraining order. The divorce didn't cause his behavior.

I got through to the judge that time. She gave me a permanent restraining order that day. We now communicate through lawyers, which is expensive, and he still gets to me through my sons who tell me when he says bad things about me – which is a lot. I know he drives by my house almost every night. I've seen his pick-up truck.

Dr. Pat: Do you feel safe?

Stephanie: Yeah. I think he drives by to see if I'm living with a man. He's a creep, and he thinks he can get out of paying me the alimony he owes if I'm living with someone, which I'm not. I have a boyfriend who sometimes stays overnight, but Jake doesn't live with me and I'm not ever remarrying. I like my freedom.

Dr. Pat: It's important for all of you to have a safety plan in mind, in case you need it, just as you did when you first separated. For a narcissistic sociopath, any time they feel they've lost control of you or the court orders them to do something, could be a time they lash out. It is all about power and control and "winning." How about you, Sharon?

Sharon: I guess I have the most contact of all of us. I still feel like I'm being abused and stalked on a regular basis.

Dr. Pat: I'm so sorry to hear that, Sharon. Unfortunately, it's common for an abuser to continue to abuse after a separation and divorce. A great deal of data suggests the first weeks and months after a separation from an abuser are the most dangerous time for violence. We now know that for someone like you, the abuse continues for years after the separation and divorce, especially when alimony and child support are involved. He won't let go.

Sharon, your children were younger at the time of your divorce. What were their ages?

Sharon: My son was eight and my daughter was six years old at the time our divorce was final. I was a stay-at-home mom and the court awarded alimony for ten years. Also, the court ordered him to pay child support and we had joint custody at first. So, we had a lot of contact then, and we still do. My son is in his first year of college and my daughter, who is in high school, is home with me. She visits him each week for dinner and he and I alternate going to the kids' therapist. For the last year he decided on his own to reduce the alimony by half when my son turned 18. I need that money! It's like he's daring me to go to court about this.

Dr. Pat: That's exactly right. He still wants to hurt you. How does contact with him make you feel?

Sharon: I feel abused! He micromanaged me during our marriage and he still tries to control everything. He's a bully. I thought it would get better. We're supposed to use the app called Our Family Wizard (OFW)[3], which might have worked, but he still calls, emails, and texts me all the time. He drives by my house every single day. He's not supposed to do any of this!

---

3   Our Family Wizard is a secure online app for co-parenting communication, including schedules, records, and secure messaging. (*www.ourfamilywizard.com*)

In the beginning, he dragged me back to court for every little thing, and I had to go back to my lawyer to respond to his nonsense. He is rich; he was fired from his big executive job a few years ago, but he got a golden parachute. I think the company wanted to get rid of him. I just got my first job since the divorce last fall, and I don't make a lot of money. Yet I have to keep paying my lawyer.

Dr. Pat: It sounds like he's still obsessed with you. He uses the court system to try to hurt and control you. He emails and texts you in violation of the court's order. He drives by your house to make you think about him. The name for this is **post separation abuse**[4]. Is he remarried?

Sharon: No, but I think he's had girlfriends. My kids told me he had a lady there when they visited him early after the divorce. I'm dating a great guy now. My ex probably knows that from my kids, and I imagine it makes him crazy. I haven't gone back to court about the alimony he owes me or his constant emails and texts. I don't want to poke the bear. I placate him so I don't have to think how dangerous he is. Years ago, during the divorce, he let me know he has a gun.

---

4   Post Separation Abuse: To maintain control and power after a relationship ends, abusers often manipulate the court system and weaponize children, friends, and family.

Dr. Pat: He is truly a sociopath, and he has not changed. You have changed. He's angry because you won't be his victim anymore, you have a new relationship, and you're on your way to healing—away from him. He still wants to get control of you. He wants to punish you. I advise you to have as little contact with him as possible. Take time to pause, think and then decide whether you need to respond or not. If it isn't essential, do not respond to his every whim and demand. There is a term called **gray rock**[5] which basically means you learn to become completely unemotional when dealing with him. You almost become boring by becoming emotionally detached. You virtually act like a rock. Emotional detachment will undermine a narcissist's attempts to lure and manipulate, and he may grow uninterested and bored. The gray rock method is recommended when you have children with a narcissist and can't maintain zero contact because of the ongoing need to communicate.

Dr. Pat: What topics do you suggest for the next time we meet?

---

5   The gray rock method is where you deliberately act unresponsive or unengaged so an abusive person will lose interest in you. Abusive people thrive on emotion and drama. When you act indifferent and don't show your emotions, they may lose interest and stop bothering you.

Sharon: Children and money.

Stephanie: I agree—children and money. And dating.

Renee: I sometimes get stuck on regrets. I'd like to talk about that.

Debbie: And planning for the future.

Dr. Pat: Got it. And let's also talk about how you got stronger. 'Till next time . . .

Dr. Pat's Notes on Contact with the EX

- Unfortunately, it's common for an abuser to continue the abuse after a separation and divorce. Data suggests the first weeks and months after a separation from an abuser are the most dangerous time for violence. The name for this is **post separation abuse.**
- It's important to have a safety plan in mind, both during and after the separation and divorce.
- Regarding contact, there is no right or wrong, as long as you're careful about safety and not becoming entangled again.
- You need to remember why you left him in the first place, so you don't get sucked back into the relationship.
- If he contacts you, take time to pause, think and then decide whether you need to respond. If it isn't essential, do not acknowledge his every whim and demand.
- The term **gray rock** basically means you learn to become completely unemotional when dealing with him.

- Your emotional detachment will undermine a narcissist's attempts to lure and manipulate. He may grow uninterested and bored with you.
- The bottom line: Have as little contact with him as possible.

Children and Finances

Dr. Pat: Hello, everyone! Good to see you again. Last time we met, you suggested we talk about children and finances. Let me start by saying alimony, child support payments and child custody always keep divorced couples entangled. This is a challenge even when there's goodwill, or at least not open hostility.

A divorce settlement helps structure responsibilities of the former spouses and minimizes future conflict—if it works. In toxic marriages, it often doesn't work. Unless you can do without alimony and your kids are adults, you'll need strategies to defang, to the extent possible, your dealings with an abusive former spouse. When parenting with a narcissistic sociopath it isn't possible to co-parent. At best, you can do **parallel parenting**.[6]

But even if you don't rely on alimony and your children are adults, the effects of an abusive marriage remain. You suffered psychological, emotional, and possibly physical

---

6 **Parallel parenting** is a method of shared parenting in which parents interact as little as possible with each other while maintaining relationships with their children. This can be an effective method when you and your ex have trouble maintaining a civil relationship.

trauma, and we know now about the long-term effects on your psyche and body. *The Body Keeps the Score*[7] is an excellent reference book about physical and mental impacts of all kinds of trauma.

For each of you, your children witnessed everything: how you were treated and how you coped. Also, what are the long-term effects for your kids, whatever their age? He's no longer your husband, but he's still their father.

SHARON

Dr. Pat: Sharon, your kids were young when you divorced. How are they doing and what's your relationship with them now?

Sharon: I thought I'd be finished dealing with my ex after the divorce. I thought all we had to do was follow the steps set down by the court and I wouldn't have to be subjected to his insults and criticisms. I was so wrong.

My kids, Sarah and Sean, were six and eight when we finally divorced. Now Sean is almost 19 and Sarah is 16. I love them so much. Sean just started college. I was awarded

---

[7] Van Der Kolk, Bessel. *The Body Keeps the Score*, New York: Penguin Group, 2014

alimony and child support in the divorce and we shared legal and physical custody. That meant certain days and nights were at my ex's house and holidays and summers were split.

At first, he was Disney Dad, a term I learned from you, Pat. He stocked a video game room in his house and took the kids on vacations. But he had little oversight of them. The kids came back to me unwashed, hadn't changed clothes or brushed their teeth, and were full of junk food. Also, they were exhausted. From what I could figure out, they had no rules with their father. At first, they thought this was great. When they returned home to me, they acted out, talking back to me and slamming doors. I was the bad parent if I said anything about their behavior. That was awful. Based on what they told me, I also suspected some inappropriate touching.

Dr. Pat: I remember you described him wrapping his whole body around your kids as a sort of hug, and even sleeping with the younger one.

Sharon: Yeah, the kids reported he still did that sometimes even though the judge told him to "knock off" this kind of touching. Apparently, it still happened. Thank goodness my son and daughter were in court ordered therapy. As time went on, things didn't work well when the kids went to his house. Shared custody worked less and less. The kids would literally run away from his house and tell me how drunk he was and how he neglected them. I had to call the police twice to intervene.

Debbie: How awful. What happened?

Sharon: I filed for full custody. I dreaded antagonizing him and I could barely pay my lawyer—I'm on a payment plan—but I had to do it for my children. My ex was awful in court. He lied and lied about what a bad parent I was. He accused me of "parental alienation." His lawyer went on and on about that. He actually told the court my ex should have full custody!

The court appointed a guardian ad litem[8] to investigate and represent the kids. The stress almost killed me. She interviewed everyone—the kids' therapist, the school, me and my ex, and the children themselves. She agreed with me that he was an unsafe parent. The judge accepted her report and awarded me full legal custody, but he still has visitation.

---

8   **Guardian ad litem**: A neutral person appointed by the court to investigate what solutions would be in the best interests of a person. During a divorce or parental rights and responsibilities case, the GAL advises about the best interests of a child.

The app Our Family Wizard (OFW) is supposed to be the only way we communicate about the kids, but he still calls, texts, and emails me all the time, criticizing everything. As I said before, he continues to drive by my house every day. He's not supposed to do any of this. I think he's crazy. He will not comply with court orders. The stress continues.

Dr. Pat: Narcissistic sociopaths hate being told what to do even when ordered by a court. They will challenge, disregard, and chip away at any order from a judge if a ruling doesn't go their way. Their goal is to win, even though it's not a contest. They don't care about the costs to others, even their children. I'm glad the Judge didn't buy the parental alienation accusation against you. It's a common assertion by angry spouses with children, but is seldom justified.

Richard Gardner, a psychiatrist, discussed this behavior in the 1980s as a dynamic in some high conflict divorces. According to Gardner, one parent will use many tactics, such as lies and scary stories, to manipulate a child into feeling fearful or hostile toward the other parent. This can happen, of course, but isn't as common as is sometimes thought.

Sharon: I didn't alienate either of my children from my ex. He does it himself. Sarah still goes out to dinner once a week with her father and we alternate taking her to therapy. Last week, Sarah told me her father was drunk, yelled at her, and then wanted Sarah to sit on his lap so he could tell her he was sorry. Sarah told me she refused to get on his lap—she's sixteen years old! I insisted on taking Sarah to her next therapy appointment even though it wasn't my turn. My ex was in the parking lot looking for us. I happened to have my friend's car, so he didn't see us. I hate this!

Dr. Pat: It is absolutely imperative that your kids continue seeing a therapist to help them understand they are not the problem. A therapist will remind them how to be safe, what to do if they're in danger, and how to recognize when they are being manipulated when your ex blames you. The therapist can also contact authorities as a mandated reporter of child abuse if there is abuse. Hopefully, your older son, Sean, can have some appointments over the summer when he's back from college.

How is your relationship with your children now?

Sharon: I love them to pieces. They're teenagers and want to be cool and seem unaffected by the turmoil in their home lives, but they come to me with their problems. They tell me about stuff at school and with their friends. We love telling goofy jokes at my house. I can't afford to shower them with vacations and luxuries. My budget is tight, but we still have movie night at home, and I can be silly and affectionate which makes them roll their eyes. But I think they like it—right?

Dr. Pat: I'm sure they do. Your kids know you love and care about them. That's the most important thing. They're safe with you. It must be a relief for them to just be themselves. But your ex will always be their father and capable of blowing things up. So, they'll probably need therapists for a long time. You mentioned being on a tight budget. Tell us more.

Sharon: I'd be fine if my ex complied with alimony and child support. About a year ago he decided to reduce the alimony he pays me. I need that money to pay our household bills for the house his own children live in. And he often subtracted money from the child support if he disagreed with an expense for the kids. And he disagreed a lot, along with calling me names for spending "his money." He challenges me so much about what I buy for the kids, like new jackets or sports equipment. He even says I take them to too many doctors. They need braces, for crying out loud. According to my lawyer he was fired from his executive job two years ago, but he received a golden parachute in the millions of dollars.

Dr. Pat: You know, Sharon, it's not really about the money. It's about control and making your life miserable. That is his MO and is, unfortunately, part of the playbook for a narcissistic sociopath ex-husband and father. He's daring you to go back to court, which for you means money and time. It also means he remains the center of your attention. You need to set and keep boundaries to protect yourself from him.

Sharon: That's easier said than done. He knocks down any barrier I set up.

Dr. Pat: Boundaries are essential and they work only if you adhere to them and repeat, repeat, repeat. Try to keep every exchange on OFW, because that can be an evidentiary record you can submit in court. Have a set reply, something like "I am following the judge's orders" and nothing more. Do not argue no matter what he says or does. If necessary, direct him to consult his attorney who will contact your attorney. Do not respond to his phone calls, texts or emails, but definitely save them. I suggest blocking him. In your own mind, keep telling yourself his behavior is way out of line. Raise a shield to his abuse. Your power is to emotionally disengage. Remember, be like a gray rock as much as possible. The only way to win with a narcissist is not to play!

Dr. Pat's Notes

- Narcissistic sociopaths hate being told what to do even, when ordered by a court. They will challenge, disregard, and chip away at any order from a judge that doesn't go their way. Their goal is to win, even though it's not a contest.
- This is not really about money. It's about control and making your life miserable. Unfortunately, this is a common part of the playbook for a narcissistic sociopath ex-husband and father.
- Firm boundaries are essential and they work only if you adhere to them and repeat, repeat, repeat. Try to keep every exchange on OFW. Have a set reply, something like "I am following the judge's orders" and nothing more.

STEPHANIE

Dr. Pat: Stephanie, your sons were teenagers during the divorce, right? Tell us about them.

Stephanie: I have two sons. Things are okay with Brian, my older son. He's 27 now, in the Coast Guard and stationed hours away. After high school he went to college, but he flunked out. He's usually respectful to me, but not always. He looks like my ex and has his voice, which sometimes freaks me out. When Brian was a little boy, he worshiped his father. That's long gone, but I wonder how he feels. I see Brian now at holidays which are usually at my sister's house and when he comes home to visit a few times a year. His drinking problem is apparent when he comes home and goes out with high school friends.

Brian is judgmental about people. I told him once not to be so critical, and he got mad at me. He shouted, "I am not Dad!" and then went on and on about what I did or didn't do right as he was growing up. I won't correct him anymore.

Brian has told me the awful things his father says about me. I don't ever start these conversations, but over the years, he has wanted to talk. So, I say "Why would he say that to you? It's not your fault. You shouldn't have to hear that stuff." I had to practice this like you told me to, Pat. What I really wanted to do was go back into the terrible details of what his father did to me, but you told me that wouldn't be good for either of us. I do enjoy being with Brian now. I wish I saw more of him.

Dr. Pat: You can let him vent because he sees you as a safe person. But try not to be abusive in comments about your ex. Saying less about your ex makes it more your son's responsibility to come to terms with who his father is—not based on your criticism of his father, but rather on his own experience with his father. Just be supportive and listen to your son's need to vent. It can be hard if Brian resembles his father, talks like him, and even has some of the same mannerisms. But he's not your ex, he's your son. What about Evan?

Stephanie: Evan is awful to me. He's 24 now. He calls me a stupid bitch all the time, just like his father did. He lives with my ex and my ex's girlfriend. Evan also works for his father's side business. He must get an earful of negative comments about me. My ex owes me a ton of alimony. I had to get a lawyer and file a contempt complaint against him. The hearing is next month, which I dread. If only I'd known enough when I got divorced to have the court order that child support and alimony were wage garnished.[9]

---

9   **Wage garnishment** is a legal procedure in which a person's earnings are required by court order to be withheld by an employer for payment of a debt, such as child support or alimony.

Sharon: Your lawyer didn't get wage garnishment? Oh, boy, that's so difficult for you, Stephanie.

Dr. Pat: Yes, it seems wage garnishment should be an automatic court order, especially with narcissistic sociopaths who want control at all costs. You'd get your alimony or child support and the ex wouldn't be reminded every time he wrote the check that he was paying you. And the ex couldn't change the amount he pays you because he disagrees with something you've done.

But narcissistic sociopaths prefer being in control of whether they write you that check. By not garnishing wages, you're handing your ex a monthly opportunity to exercise power and control over you. And in your case Stephanie, he just stopped paying for over a year, right?

Stephanie: Actually, about three years. Yeah, I wish my attorney had made sure of that for me. And the situation is complicated by my son Evan asking me, "Why are you so mean to Dad? Stop picking on us. You don't need any alimony. You have a job. You are a stupid bitch to be taking Dad to court for money. You should be ashamed." Blah blah blah.

This really hurts because Evan was at home and saw how terrible and violent his father was to me before we separated, and afterward too—verbally and physically abusive. I'm pretty sure Evan and his father are both alcoholics. Thanksgiving and Christmas at my sister's house are tense. I make it a point to never talk about their father—ever. No one in my family mentions my ex at all.

Last Christmas, Evan was quiet for a while and then blew up at the dinner table when I mentioned the price of groceries going up. He called me stupid and ridiculous, and said I waste money. I don't waste money! Then he stormed out of my sister's house. I was up all night crying and stressing about his treatment of me and worrying he'd be in an accident on his way home. The next day, Evan tried to get in my house—I don't know why. I had the locks changed a few months ago. I've had to change the locks a few times over the years. His old key didn't work, so he tried to bash the door in. He's just like his father.

Dr. Pat: Your ex is clearly using Evan to get to you. He tells Evan terrible lies about you and blames you for everything. He wants to estrange Evan from you because he knows that will hurt you. He also wants to show the world he's such a good father that his son wants to live with him.

Stephanie: My own son hates me. My own son abuses me. What did I do wrong?

Dr. Pat: That is the wrong question. The real question is: Why does your ex use his son to abuse you? The answer is, because your ex is an abuser and will not change. He weaponized his son against you, knowing how much pain it causes. This is called **Abuse by Proxy** and is tragically common in situations like yours. It's a lot worse than **Parental Alienation.** These abusers care only about themselves and don't even mind if their own kids suffer. There's no rising above the situation for them. It's always about them and their desire to win and continue hurting you. Your ex is using Evan to get to you.

Stephanie: What can I do? People tell me what a great young man Evan is out in public. He seems to save his anger for me. Although, come to think of it, Evan is abusive to his girlfriend. Wow! It's scary how much Evan acts just like his Dad. It's not getting any better with Evan. I raised the boys and I want a good relationship with them. I love them!

Dr. Pat: To Evan and anyone else who comments on legal matters such as alimony, simply say—if you care to respond: "There's a court order on alimony," and leave it at that. As

I've said before, the technique of gray rock can be used with adult children, too.

Stephanie: Okay. But my heart is broken about Evan.

Dr. Pat: I understand how that must hurt, Stephanie. But you must remember you've been a good mother to both your boys. It's sad that Evan has taken on your ex's abusive behavior, but you must set and keep boundaries. You and I have talked about this before. Whenever Evan is disrespectful or calls you names, state calmly that you love him, but he cannot treat you like that. Then walk away. If he's abusive during a phone call, tell him you're hanging up, and do it. He may erupt more, but it's important for you to set these boundaries.

If you feel you're in danger, call 911. If you can record any of these incidents, do so. Of course, you love your son and you want him to love you. Do not feel guilty about this. You did not cause his abusive behavior toward you. I know you don't want to hear this, but you may need to break off relations with your son when he yells at you again. This is the hardest thing for any mother to do, but it might be necessary. You once told me your sister dreads having Evan come over and doesn't want to include him anymore for holidays. This is a natural consequence of his behavior.

You may even need a protective order against him. I know that's the hardest part, but you don't deserve being called names by your son or anyone else. And if you let him do it and keep hoping again and again that next time he'll suddenly become a kind and loving son, you are enabling his abuse. You're giving him more opportunities to mistreat you and call you names. He is responsible for his own behavior, although he should get a lot of therapy for his anger issues. Has he had therapy?

Stephanie: He met with a counselor in high school a few times during the divorce. I don't think he's had therapy since then.

Dr. Pat: Could you suggest it?

Stephanie: No way! He'd blow up at me and call me a stupid bitch who thinks something is wrong with him. He says all the time that I'm the crazy one. In his mind, I'm guilty of everything bad in our family. He also refers to therapists as Dr. Do Nothings and a waste of time and money. Just like how his father talks about counselors.

Dr. Pat: Okay. Let it be. You don't want to provoke more abuse. Someday, maybe Evan will seek professional help, but that won't happen if he keeps deluding himself that nothing is wrong with him.

Dr. Pat's Notes

- I believe wage garnishment should be an automatic court order, especially with narcissistic sociopaths who want control at all costs.
- By not garnishing wages, you hand your ex a monthly opportunity to exercise power and control over you.
- When your ex weaponizes children to abuse you, this is called Abuse by Proxy and is tragically common in relationships with sociopathic narcissists.
- Don't hesitate to use the gray rock technique with abusive adult children.
- If a child or adult child takes on your ex's abusive behavior, you must set and keep boundaries. If you feel you're in danger, call 911. If you can record any of these incidents, do so.
- Do not feel guilty about this. You did not cause the abusive behavior.
- You may need a protective order against an abusive adult child. I know it's terribly hard, but if you let it go on, you're enabling the abuse and making yourself a target. Adults should be responsible for their own behavior.

RENEE

Dr. Pat: Renee, what about your kids?

Renee: Thankfully, my four children were already adults during the divorce, so we had no custody or child support issues. In the divorce settlement my ex had to continue paying their college loans for two years after the divorce, and I took over after that. He played games throughout the two years by always paying late and causing us to get notices of late payment. As for contact, none of them to my knowledge, has any contact with their father, who lives close by. They each told him to leave them alone, and he has, as far as I know.

This isn't surprising, because he had little or no relationship with them when they were growing up. He was never home. He'd come home from work after they were in bed and was still asleep when they left for school. I was busy raising four children and started working again when they all reached school age.

Life with him was crazy hectic. Now I think that was part of the cover for his disgusting secret life. The only attention they got from him was when they were in a sporting event or a play. He did attend those. But if they weren't performing, he was MIA—missing in action. It was almost like they only interested him when he could brag about them, like, "Look at my kid on the soccer field! Aren't I great to have a kid like that?" It was never about what was good for the children.

Dr. Pat: Narcissists use their children in public to show what great parents they are. They see their kids' accomplishments as an extension of themselves. Did your children have therapy?

Renee: Yes, all of them went to therapy during the almost four-year divorce ordeal and my two sons are still in therapy. One son is having an especially hard time finding his path in life. He's gone through several jobs and took more courses after college. I'm proud of him for getting his degree, and I tell him so. But he has a drinking problem.

My kids deserved a loving, involved father. They didn't have one, and that's painful for me—but it's on their father, not them. My middle son recently told me he's terrified of becoming like his dad. That was a surprise because we almost never mention their father. I assured him that was impossible for many reasons because my son is a generous, helpful person and has empathy. I left unsaid that those qualities are a stark contrast to his narcissist father, who is selfish, cold, and cruel.

Dr Pat: Good. Don't dump on the father. And believe me I understand how difficult that can be. But try hard to zip it when it comes to putting down their dad in front of your kids. That is rule number one, because otherwise, your kids are stuck in a storm they didn't create. And that can backfire.

Your children, Renee, see him for what he is. To all of you, please know that while your kids inherited some features from your exes, they are very different people. As for the drinking, it's not uncommon for children of alcoholics to become alcoholics too. Drinking or drugs sedate the emotional pain.

Your kids, Renee, have the pain of a mostly neglectful father who lied to the whole family throughout their lives about what he was doing. He wasn't just unfaithful to you— he was unfaithful to the entire family. They also saw his hyper-critical behavior toward you. You told us he would insult your cooking, your religion, how you dressed and even how you spoke. He also enjoyed gaslighting you.

Gaslighting is a type of psychological abuse often used by narcissistic sociopaths to sow seeds of doubt in the victim, making them question their memories, perceptions, and judgment. People who experience gaslighting often feel confused and anxious, or as though they can't trust themselves.

Your kids saw how run down you were and how you tried to cope by minimizing friction in the house. They witnessed it all, including the family's eruption when their father gave you an STD. That's a lot of trauma for the kids, no matter their age.

What about now?

Renee: I feel close to each of them. Two live across the state, but we talk, text or visit often. We're usually together for holidays and birthdays. We all spend a few summer days at a cabin I rent with my sister's family. You told me once to create a new family with myself and my four children. That's what I've tried to do since the divorce.

My daughter has a baby now, and I help a lot. We close our conversations saying, "I love you." After the divorce I spoke to each one and apologized profusely for selecting the ex to be their father. At the time, you told me to tell them I was so glad they're my children and I love them. I did say that. I also told them, while I can't change the past, I can look forward, love them, and be a good mom. And I've tried to be a loving mother.

If I dwelt on the past I'd go completely crazy, so I try not to think about it, except when I'm here with a professional psychologist. I know I'm lucky to have good relationships with my kids.

Dr. Pat: That isn't luck. You escaped abuse by proxy because your kids didn't let it happen. They stayed away from their father. That can be seen as tragic in some global sense that they have no relationship with him, but keeping away protected them and is a perfectly acceptable way to deal with a toxic person—who just happens to be their biological father.

What about finances?

Renee: I had a final money settlement, so I didn't get alimony. I wanted to break all ties with him. I'm a lot poorer than when we had a two-income family, but I make it work.

Dr. Pat: You're fortunate not to have alimony or child support, because you can have no contact with the ex.

Dr. Pat's Notes

Narcissists use their children in public to show what great parents they are. They see their kids' accomplishments as an extension of themselves.

While your kids inherited some features from your exes, they are very different people. As for drinking, it isn't uncommon for children of alcoholics to become alcoholics too. Drinking or drugs sedate the emotional pain.

Gaslighting[10] is a type of psychological abuse often used by narcissistic sociopaths to sow seeds of doubt in the victim, making them question their memories, perceptions, and judgment. People who experience gaslighting often feel confused and anxious, or as though they can't trust themselves.

If your kids want to avoid contact with their dad, that's a perfectly acceptable way to deal with a toxic person who just happens to biologically be their father.

---

10 There are four primary types of gaslighting behaviors: the straight-up lie, reality manipulation, scapegoating and coercion.

DEBBIE

Dr. Pat: Debbie, how are your kids?

Debbie: Like Renee, I didn't have custody issues even though my two daughters were still teenagers during the divorce. My ex was not an involved father and never asked for joint custody or visitation. Our divorce was only about the house and the business. Mia, my younger daughter, used to call her father from time to time to chat, but he's not a chatter. She told me he never called her. I don't think she calls him anymore, and I never bring up their dad. She was hurt by him. My other daughter, Jeanie, was very angry at the time and after the divorce. She refused to see him or even talk about him.

Dr. Pat: How old are your daughters now?

Debbie: 28 and 25.

Dr. Pat: What's your relationship with them now? How often do you see them?

Debbie: They both live at home with me!

Dr. Pat: Really? Tell us about that.

Debbie: My younger daughter Mia moved back with me about six years ago. She struggled with jobs and life in general when she had her own apartment. I was helping all the time. When she asked to come back and live at home, I said yes. She helps with household chores and volunteers with me. She's a quiet and anxious person. I worry about her.

Dr. Pat: What about your other daughter?

Debbie: Jeanie was full of rage during and after the divorce. Some of that was directed at me. She told me recently that all she remembers about the divorce was seeing me on the phone all the time. She felt neglected. That hurt, for sure. I guess I was on the phone a lot, because I was in the middle of a contentious divorce and the business was crumbling.

Dr. Pat: She lives with you also?

Debbie: Yes. Jeanie went to community college, got a job, and moved into an apartment. Then she got married! I gave her a nice wedding at a restaurant in the country. They bought a house and moved three hours away. Honestly, I didn't see much of her after that. The marriage didn't even last two years. No children, thank goodness. About six months ago she asked to come back home until she could sort things out, and I said yes. I am definitely not an empty nester!

Dr. Pat: You're right about that! Living with adult children is a challenge. Be clear about house rules and expectations. I hope you know your girls are back with you because they feel safe with you. They love you.

Debbie: Thanks, I need to hear that. And I do set some ground rules. But I have to admit it's good to have my kids with me. Maybe we can use this time together as healing years.

Dr. Pat: That sounds perfect, Debbie. Look at these years with your girls as a time to bond and develop healthy family ties. It may take them longer to mature, but in time they may be ready to go out and live on their own.

Dr. Pat's Notes

- Living with adult children can be a challenge. Be clear about house rules and expectations.
- Look at this as a time to bond and develop healthy family ties.
- Your children will look to you as a safe person. You can create a new family life with love, security, and new traditions.

Dr. Pat's Notes About Children and Finances

Let's see if I can summarize and give you some advice:

There's only so much any of you can do. Some of your kids are alcoholics or becoming problem drinkers. I recommend Alcoholics Anonymous. I recommend Al Anon for the other kids and for you as well.

Stephanie, your son, Evan, is an abuser, and is mostly beyond your control. You need to continue trying to set boundaries with him. By living with his father, he continues to learn bad behavior patterns. He's not only abusing you, but his girlfriend as well. We can hope that someday this pattern will be broken, but it isn't something you can make happen.

Mainly, for all of you, your kids need to know you love them. Also, it's great for them to see you getting on with your life in a positive and healthy way. The more you live a healthy, productive life the better off they will be as well. They all look to you as their safe person. Even when Evan is abusing you Stephanie, I think he is really acting out his personal rage. I hope he gets some therapy someday.

Remember, each one of **you** can create a new life for yourself, and **you** can create a new family life. How you live your life, the family traditions you begin, the love you show your children, even your adult children, has a tremendous impact on them. You are the family now.

You are in control!

Dating or Not Dating

Dr. Pat: What are you doing about dating? We know the singles scene has dramatically changed since you dated your exes.

SHARON

Sharon: About a year after my divorce, I began dating a nice guy named Jay. My ex looked him up on social media and found out Jay had another girlfriend, Karen, who was a pediatrician. Jay and I weren't serious, and I already knew he had this other relationship. We were more like friends with benefits. He was a big outdoorsman and I liked that.

Anyway, Jay died suddenly of a heart attack. My ex then contacted Jay's other girlfriend Karen and told her Jay was unfaithful to her with me. My ex is a sick, cruel man.

A couple of years ago I met Jerry, the man I'm now dating. He is a good, kind man with a steady job in the landscaping business. In fact, my ex and I first met him when we had work done on our house after moving to the area. Jerry doesn't drink or smoke. He's a naturalist and kind of a health nut. He loves being outdoors. On most of our dates we go hiking or skiing.

Dr. Pat: Does your ex torment Jerry? Is Jerry afraid of your ex?

Sharon: Fortunately, not at all. Jerry is strong, athletic and confident. And since he met the ex a long time ago while doing landscaping work on the house, Jerry already knew my ex as a bully and a jerk. I'm letting Jerry into my life a little at a time. I'm stronger now, but I have to be careful. I think I'm in love!

Dr. Pat, Debbie, Stephanie and Renee cheer and tell Sharon they're happy for her.

DEBBIE

Debbie: I actually dated a lot at first. The whole online dating scene was a hoot, especially when my friend, Denise, and I set up our profile pages. We drank some wine and laughed a lot. We took head shots of each other trying to look as friendly and as pretty as we could muster. After a few days we checked on the responses, and selected some guys to meet. I always met in a public place, and never gave out my home address. I was careful not to be followed.

The procedure after you get some responses is to decide who to text, then maybe talk with the guy on the phone. If that goes well, you might set up a time and place to meet. A lot of these guys just wanted sex. It was disgusting. I had some rules.

Dr. Pat: Like what?

Debbie: The man had to be single, a widower, divorced, or in the last stages of a divorce.

Dr Pat: That's a good dating rule, but tell me why from your point of view?

Debbie: I'm not a home wrecker. I will not cause a family to blow up because of me. My ex cheated on me and I was shattered. I won't do that to another woman. I will also not be some man's side dish.

Dr. Pat: Yes, it seems to me that women who cheat with married men, are betraying other women. They're not part of the female tribe that supports one another. Also, if he's lying to his wife and kids and he's good at it, he will lie to you. So, not a great person to date.

Debbie: Agreed. I also want to keep things light on the first date – mostly talk about each other's interests and jobs. That's the first rule for me. I do not want to hear about the guy's horrible wife. In fact, I would ask him to tell me one good thing about his ex. That's Rule #2 for me. The answer was usually about her being a good mother, and that's okay.

You mentioned lying. I was truthful in my profile, but these guys lie all the time in their bios.

Sharon: What do they lie about? What grades they got in college?

Debbie: No, stuff like their height, weight, age, and occupation. Most say how great they are at satisfying a woman – which, of course, must be why they're looking for dates online!

Sharon: Wait. You said they lie about their age and height? You will meet the guy – right?

Debbie: Exactly! I have a funny story about that one. My friend Denise is ten years older than I am, a widow, and she's a complete blast. We thought we'd jump into the dating pool together. We both felt ready.

When we arranged our first dates, I felt nervous as heck and so did Denise. Anyway, we each had guys who looked interesting respond to our profile pages, and we arranged it so we had dates on the same night, near each other. We would go to different restaurants, but park in the same parking lot. We were giggling like schoolgirls. I bought a new outfit.

My date said he was 36, which was, ahem, younger than me, but he knew my age and his other info looked intriguing. I walked into the restaurant, which had a bar and a dining room. I scanned the room and didn't see anyone, so I sat at the bar thinking he was running late. Then a very young man came over and introduced himself. He was my date? He kinda' looked like his photo. He was all smiles and all I could stammer out was "How old are you?" He said he was 23, and he was sorry he told a fib, but he didn't think I'd go out on a date with him if he told his real age . . . and who cares about age anyway ... and he finds me so attractive ... and he thinks older women are great ... and he hopes I'm okay with this, and all this time my brain is screaming – I DON'T DATE CHILDREN!

When he finished talking, I told him I had children his age, and he told me that was okay with him. I excused myself to go to the restroom where I quickly texted Denise. She had already texted me that her date was over and she'd be waiting for me in the parking lot.

I said good-bye to the boy with mommy issues, and walked briskly to my car, where Denise was leaning against it with her head in her hands. I asked if she was okay. She said her date, who said that he was 63 years old, was AT LEAST 80 years old, and he started their conversation wanting to talk about politics.

We burst out laughing and drove to a neighborhood restaurant for pizza to salvage our night out.

Renee: I'm laughing too, but what an ordeal! How many online dates did you go on?

Debbie: Hard to say. I didn't look on the dating site again for a couple of weeks, but a mixture of boredom and wanting to feel wanted got me back in. Young people meet interesting people on line all the time. I figured I just had to get some experience. But my feelings are mixed. Online dating is a marketplace of lonely people. It can make me feel deflated. My goal was to meet a good person, who was interesting, with good values and a sense of humor. Instead, I had a bunch of ridiculous dates over five or six years.

Stephanie: You had other ridiculous dates?

Debbie: Oh yes, I did. Pat told me to keep a journal of my dating adventures, which I did. It was therapeutic to write things down!

Dr. Pat: Right now, I want to follow up on the longer-term relationship you mentioned rather than the dating disasters.

Debbie: Okay. Yes, I did finally meet an interesting man. An acquaintance introduced us at a restaurant after I stopped by to say hi to her. She knew a customer who was there by himself. I think it was a coincidence. She introduced us. He was a regular, she said. We sat at the bar for a little while and exchanged phone numbers. He was handsome and long divorced, with two adult sons. We got to know each other and ended up dating for about a year. It was fun, and I hadn't had fun in a long, long time. It felt great!

Then he became more distant and controlling. We broke up when he told me I was too independent and selfish. He seemed to want all my attention. He wanted me to be so grateful for every thoughtful thing he did for me, and he was clear, almost adamant, that he was there to take care of me. I loved the flowers he sent me, the candy on Valentine's Day, and all the kind things he did for me. I said thank you a lot! He could be very sweet. But I have a life. I have friends and sometimes I would work at my friend's restaurant and I had to work late. He didn't like it if I ever had to change our plans.

He was becoming rigid. He wanted to know my schedule every day. I started to feel suffocated, and I knew this wasn't a good feeling. It was starting to bother me. You were right, Pat, about dating a guy for a good long time to see how they react to different circumstances.

Dr. Pat: When did you know for sure?

Debbie: Our last date was at his house. Our relationship was sort of superficial. It was fun going out to dinner, to the movies, concerts, basketball games, even watching television and such. But I wanted to learn more about his background and his feelings, or else end the relationship. After dinner, we were chatting about all kinds of things, with me doing most of the talking as usual. I invited him to a friend's Super Bowl party the next day. He told me he was going to visit his son at college for lunch, but he'd be back later in the day and could meet me at the party. I said great, and to call when he got home.

Then I asked more about his son. He clammed up as always. I don't think he would have even mentioned visiting his son if I hadn't said there was a Super Bowl party. I never met his sons and he wouldn't ever talk about them, even though he had custody after his divorce. However, he met my daughters and most of my friends many times.

I was tired of getting dead ended like that. I waited a bit and made the excuse I had to get up in the morning for brunch with some of my friends. We hugged and kissed goodbye, and I said I'd see him at the party. It seemed okay. The next day, I didn't hear from him despite my calls and texts. I was worried he was in an accident or something. He finally texted me on Monday afternoon that he was fine, but did not want to go out with me anymore.

Well, I needed and wanted to talk about it. He did not. He finally agreed to call after he got home from work. On the phone? After a year? Really? I needed an explanation, and on the phone that night it took a lot to convince him I could withstand the hurt of our break-up (Oh, please!) and that I deserved an explanation.

He unloaded this on me: I wasn't grateful enough for what he did for me; I wasn't attentive enough to him; I cancelled plans (only one time when I had to work late, for crying out loud); I talked to my friends too long at parties to the exclusion of him (didn't I remember that party three months ago blah blah blah?); I talked too much about my own life; I was too independent, and I didn't need him enough.

He wanted someone to take care of (his words), who gushed at him (my words). He said he didn't return my calls or texts the day before to show me how it feels when I ignore him. I told him I didn't know I was being punished.

That made him mad! That was it! Over and done! How I was supposed to know ANY of that from a person who didn't communicate well is beyond me, but the red flags were flying high at that point!

After that, I have pretty much stopped trying to date. If a wonderful unattached man falls out of the sky, I'll think about it. But I'm not searching. It's been almost two years. Some people ask me "Haven't you found someone yet?" All this makes me question who I am.

Dr. Pat: Debbie, I congratulate you for trusting your gut. If you feel suffocated and controlled by someone, those are certainly warning signs of an unhealthy relationship. You don't need any more of that in your life. As to people asking if you've found anyone yet, you can have a "sound bite" or canned response ready like "Sure, I've found a lot, but none I want to keep." That will shut them up.

And by the way, it is perfectly fine to not want to date, and to be happy being on your own. Often, after leaving an abusive relationship, or having a string of dating disasters, it feels very good not answering to anyone but yourself. You are your own person, and you have every right to date or not date!

Debbie: To be honest, dating scares me now, especially online dating sites. If I initiated a contact, the guys online were asking for naked pictures of me before they would talk. When I got that first request for a naked photo, I searched online for a picture of the oldest naked woman I could find—this woman had to be 95 years old–and I sent it to the jerk who asked. He answered with an expletive. Needless to say, he wasn't anyone I'd be interested in meeting. So, it was another reason to just stop. I keep busy. I have friends. And my kids are home with me now, which makes dating feel weird for me.

Sharon: My kids are home, and my boyfriend comes over and we go out. It's not weird for me.

Dr. Pat: Many women date when their kids are still at home.

Debbie. I know, I know. But it just feels off to me somehow. Don't get me wrong, I would still like to go to the movies or out to dinner with a man sometimes, but I have another concern.

Dr. Pat: What?

Debbie: I'm afraid I'll get tangled up with another controlling guy. I feel like I dodged a bullet with the last guy.

Dr. Pat: You *did* dodge a bullet. But you dodged it because of what you know now about trusting your gut and seeing red flags.

Debbie: But I find myself kind of bored with guys who are just nice, you know?

Dr. Pat: What do you mean?

Debbie: I'm attracted to smart and confident guys, but then I see red flags waving. What does this say about me if I find nice guys boring? Dating feels forced now, like I'd be dating because my friends kept after me to do it. Now I want my own space. Am I okay? Am I arrogant and cold? Am I dysfunctional and selfish? What's wrong with me that I throw myself entirely into love with a person or not at all?

Dr. Pat: You have a lot of questions there, Debbie. But they are the thoughts and questions of many women who left a narcissistic sociopath. One thing for sure: Narcissistic sociopaths are exciting and charismatic at the beginning of a relationship. They "love bomb" you. That's what attracts you, and it's only later that you see their controlling and abusive ways. **Love bombing** is red flag in dating. This is when, early on, the person says that you're everything they've been looking for. You are their sun and moon, their soul mate. Beware! This is a narcissistic sociopath's classic way of getting in. It is a seduction technique. The initial rapid idealization is designed to lure you in, and then—as you know—in time the belittling and abuse begins.

I recommend any women who has left an abuser should take it slow in any new dating relationship. You need at least a year to get to know a person, warts and all. Anyone can fake nice for six months to a year. Only in time do you see the guy for who he is. Then you may find the exciting guy is really a pompous jerk. Debbie, you saw this firsthand with your handsome "Fun Guy." You were being cautious, and that's smart. You are taking a break—temporary or permanent—but it's on your own terms. That is empowering.

Debbie: But is it fear? When I love, all I want to do is make the other person happy. I am a fixer, but I fear I'll lose myself again in another relationship. I am always the pleaser. I didn't even see the so-called problems my boyfriend had with me. I thought he was just uptight about his kids. Then a lightbulb went on and I realized he was a selfish jerk who wanted me to fawn all over him to the exclusion of my friends. I need to find balance and take care of myself.

Dr. Pat: It's good that you realize you sometimes try to "fix" others and make others happy, often at the expense of yourself. This can lead to a codependent relationship, in that you're more concerned about what the other person wants, instead of being your authentic self, and looking at what you need and want in a relationship.

People who survive an abusive relationship need time to learn about who *they* are—what *they* love to do and what *their* goals in life are. If they do this now, then when (and if) they choose to be in a relationship, it will be a healthier give and take—a more balanced relationship. But just know there is absolutely nothing wrong with you. You are a passionate person, Debbie, and wiser now after what you've been through. YOU choose whether to be in a relationship or not. Only you.

Debbie: I used to think if I was alone, that meant I must be dysfunctional. I am finally beginning to realize it may be just fine to be on my own—to live my life free and unencumbered.

Dr. Pat's Notes

- If you feel suffocated and controlled by someone, those are warning signs of an unhealthy relationship.
- It's perfectly fine if you don't date and you're happy being on your own. Often, after leaving an abusive relationship, it feels good not answering to anyone but yourself.
- Be cautious. Narcissistic sociopaths are exciting and charismatic at the beginning of a relationship. They love bomb you. That's what attracts you, and only later do you see their controlling and abusive ways. That's one reason I recommend taking it slow with new relationships. It takes at least a year to get to know a person, warts and all. Anyone can fake nice for six months to a year. Only with time do you see a guy for who he is. Then you may find the exciting guy is actually a pompous jerk.
- If you're always the pleaser, it's good to recognize that you try to fix others and make them happy, often at your own expense. These are codependent relationships, in that you're more concerned about what the other person wants, rather than being your

authentic self, and looking at what you need and want in a relationship.

- Take time to learn about who you are—what you love to do and your goals in life. If you do this now, then in the future when (and if) you choose to be in a relationship, it will be a healthier relationship with more give and take.
- Remember, nothing is wrong with you. You are a wiser person after surviving everything that you've been through. YOU choose whether to be in a relationship or not. Only you.

STEPHANIE

Stephanie: I've got to tell you, Debbie, you're an amazing person, single or not. Don't let society tell you that you need a man, because you do not! I've been dating a guy on and off since our group met years ago. I like his company, but I don't need him.

Renee: I remember him waiting for you in the parking lot after one of our support meetings. Wow, you've been dating him a long time.

Stephanie: That's right. Bill is a nice guy and he likes me. I am absolutely clear with him that we're not headed to marriage. He used to urge me to sell my house and move in with him and the sale proceeds of my house would then be my "nest egg." I said no, as gently as I could, and he still wants to be my occasional boyfriend. I like my space, alone time, and my time with friends.

Bill's the one who told me that a white truck drives by my house about five o'clock almost every morning. My neighbor mentioned this also. I think my ex is taking videos or photos to show the judge I'm living with a man, which would affect the alimony. I am most definitely not living with Bill, although Bill would like that. He rarely stays overnight.

When I told my new attorney about my ex driving by every morning, he suggested I wake up early, and when I see the truck, turn on all the lights and hit the panic button on the car. I did that, and ex hasn't come back as far as I know. I can't wait for this hearing on the alimony he owes me to be over with. It's so stressful.

Dr. Pat: Stephanie, I remember when Bill would pressure you to sell your house and how he'd come over, even when you asked him to give you space. You've worked hard at setting boundaries with Bill and I think that's great. I don't think this relationship would've worked if Bill didn't hear your message repeatedly, loud and clear. You took charge and decided how much "Bill" you wanted in your life. He accepted your boundaries.

You made a choice early on that you didn't want to live with him, and that choice has been a lifesaver for you, Stephanie. You listened to yourself, rather than letting him pressure and control you. Good for you!

RENEE

Dr. Pat: Renee, have you dated?

Renee: No, I haven't dated at all!

Dr. Pat: Well, that's very clear. Do you want to explain?

Renee: I just don't feel the need to date. I've built a full life for myself, and I have friends. I'm not the least bit motivated to jump into the dating pool. My marriage was so fake and the divorce so cataclysmic, that I just need to concentrate on myself and trying to do some good in the world.

I need to focus all my energy on recovery from minimizing myself and my needs and wants for 27 years. Another man—no way!

Dr. Pat: That is completely fine, Renee. You don't want or need to date, and you're comfortable with that. Bravo!

Dr. Pat: I often hear from women in my practice that they aren't interested in living with another man after they're divorced or widowed. Many women think men just want someone to take care of them—cooking, cleaning, and sex. And in fact, statistics show that men tend to find another partner within a year or two after being widowed or divorced.

I think if a woman has her own means of financial support she can be as independent and free as she wants to be. Some women look to men to support them, at least financially, and that's often where problems begin. You marry for financial security, not because this is a good partner for you. So, I do recommend giving yourself time after a divorce to settle down on your own. If your life is full and then you meet a nice, kind man who is also emotionally healthy, then you may add to each other's lives.

You don't complete the other person, nor do they complete you. Rather, like a Venn diagram, you overlap and enjoy each other's company, but remain whole and complete as individuals. You give each other space, to be separate individuals, as well as enjoy time together. This is not always easy to find, so take your time and think about your needs and wants before selecting someone to be your partner.

Dr. Pat's Notes

- I often hear from women in my practice that they aren't interested in living with another man after they're divorced or widowed.
- I think if a woman has her own means of financial support she can be as independent and free as she wants. Some women look to men to support them, at least financially, and that's often where problems begin. In that case, you marry for financial security, not because this is a good partner for you.
- I recommend giving yourself time after a divorce to settle down on your own. If your life is full and then you meet a nice, kind man who is also emotionally healthy, then you may add to each other's lives.

If you've been in a relationship all your adult life, living alone can be frightening at first, even though your partner was abusive. This web page offers tips for creating a new life without a partner: https://www.healthline.com/health/how-to-live-alone.

Creating the House of Love

During 40 years doing clinical psychology work I've often been asked what makes a successful relationship. I combined some of my own ideas with the work of John and Julie Gottman of the Gottman Institute to come up with a formulation called **CREATEing the House of Love.**

I suggest you look at the components of this House of Love while dating and before you commit to marriage. Often when someone is unhappy in a marriage, I go over the House of Love components to find areas that are missing in the relationship. Almost always we find many essential components are absent. If you decide to date, I suggest you think of this helpful framework:

1. When building the house, you need a strong **Foundation.**
    - **Commitment** is the foundation, the capacity to honor and love your spouse throughout your lives and remain faithful until "death do you part."
2. When building a house, you need **Support Beams.** As a memory aid, these beams spell the word CREATE.

- **C – Chemistry:** Yes, you need to feel attracted to your partner and feel the chemistry of love. But this alone will not sustain a marriage.
- **R – Respect:** This is an important component of admiring and valuing your partner and feeling respected in return.
- **E – Enjoyment:** You need to enjoy doing things together, such as hiking, travelling, reading, going out to dinner, sports activities, etc.
- **A – Acceptance:** This means taking a good, hard look at your partner and being willing to accept that person, warts and all. Don't go into a relationship thinking you can change someone.
- **T – Trust:** This means you can count on the other person to be faithful. It also means you trust that person to "have your back" and be accountable for promises made.
- **E – Empathy** – You are both able and willing to stand in one another's shoes and feel what your partner is feeling. Remember that ALL narcissistic sociopath partners lack the capacity for empathy.

3. And last, but not least, you need a **Roof** for the House of Love. The Roof keeps your Support Beams from eroding over time. This roof is **Communication:** The ability to listen with full attention and respect and willingness to hear and feel your partner's perspective when solving problems. This ability to talk through problems is essential to healthy communication.

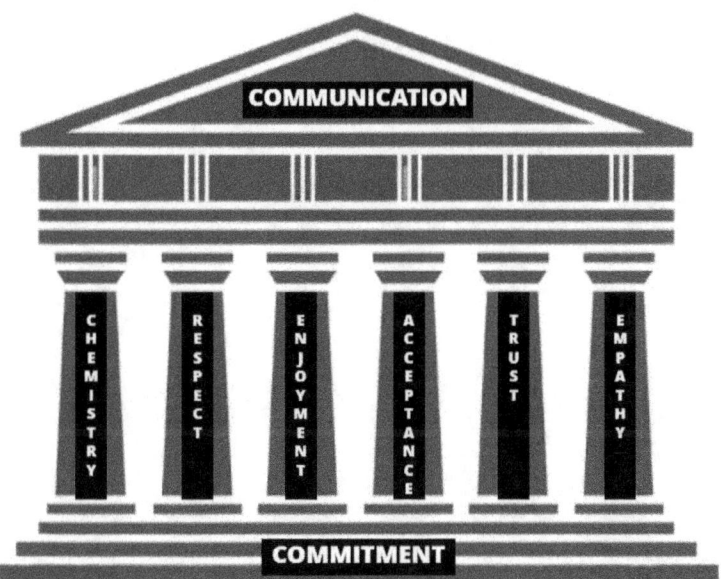

Narcissistic sociopaths cannot fulfill the above commitments over time, although they can fake it for a few months. Before long, you'll realize your relationship lacks Commitment and has never had many of the Support Beams, such as Respect, Acceptance, Trust and Empathy. In almost all cases, you will not have the necessary Roof for good Communication.

Looking Back

Never be a prisoner of your past. It was just a lesson, not a life sentence. –Unknown

Dr. Pat: Ten years have passed since each of you separated from your husbands. In every case the legal process was lengthy and stressful, but you slogged through it. Looking back and taking a long view, now that you know so much more, how do you view what happened to you?

What lessons can you share with other women who are in the early stages of separation, divorce, or its aftermath?

Renee, as the oldest member of The Group, how do you see your past with 20/20 hindsight?

RENEE

Renee: I see that I was gullible and naïve. I fell for a smart, charming man who said he would love, honor and cherish me. I believed him and couldn't wait to start a family. Although we dated for two years before getting married, I now realize I didn't know him at all. I was bamboozled!

I believed him when he said he was working late and every weekend. I didn't know a person was capable of lying, conniving and being so mean to his family. I didn't know that was even possible, so I patched together every resource I had to keep life steady at home and be a nurturing and loving partner.

Until I started therapy with you, Pat, I didn't even have the vocabulary to know I was married to a narcissistic sociopath who was a pathological liar and enjoyed gaslighting me. Therapy gave me a reality check that none of his behavior was healthy or normal. I realized my attempts to fix things by minimizing my needs played right into his game. I was actually enabling him. Ouch!

But I got out, didn't I? I have two big regrets: that I married this scoundrel and that he is the father to my children. They deserved to have a loving father. I wish I could have a do-over!

Dr. Pat: Regrets are often viewed as negative choices we shouldn't dwell on. But actually, letting yourself feel regret can be therapeutic as you move forward. If you allow yourself to feel the sadness or anger that comes with regret, then you can move into broader thinking and less self-blame. For example, you may come to accept that marrying a con artist wasn't your fault. He is a superb manipulator. Or perhaps you regret marrying him but realize that otherwise you wouldn't have your children.

These healing thoughts can help you move forward to a better life. You can learn to confront and rationally think about your regrets instead of wallowing in them. Make your regrets a catalyst toward future healthy behavior.

Believe me, we all have regrets. Anyone who says they don't is probably in denial. Regret is normal, but we shouldn't get stuck there. Feel, think, and then act. A great book by Daniel Pink is *The Power of Regret: How Looking Backward Moves Us Forward.*[11]

Regret can give us wisdom if we're willing to learn. People who say they have no regrets are usually not growing as individuals.

Renee, what other wisdom can you share from your experiences?

Renee: Hmmm . . . You're asking for wisdom from a person who was duped most of her life?

---

11 Pink, Daniel. *The Power of Regret: How Looking Backward Moves Us Forward.* New York: Riverhead Books, 2022

Dr. Pat: Yes, because you're a survivor and a super smart person. I know you've thought about this.

Renee: Actually, I think about it a lot. For life lessons, I say this: Pay attention to what your friends say about your boyfriend. In my case, my sister especially told me to be careful about him. She had a gut feeling, but I didn't listen.

If your marriage and family life isn't how you want or need it to be, do something about it sooner—not later! I wasted so many years doubting my instincts, trying to convince myself what I was experiencing wasn't so bad, and every bad episode was just a rough patch. I would think, "He's just in a bad mood or under a lot of stress. Things will get better and our family will be happy." I was so wrong.

People say: always have hope. But for me, hope was a noose that almost destroyed me. All I did was cope and hope. So, I urge anyone in a bad relationship to stop hoping and get individual counseling. You can try marriage counseling too, but I discovered my ex was incredibly manipulative in couples counseling.

Also consult a lawyer to learn your options. Set up a bank account of your own. Have a safety plan in place, and gather copies or originals of all your important documents. And take notes or keep a journal of your thoughts—in a notebook, not on your computer. You may need to hide this. Writing things down helped me vent my feelings and later helped me remember things. Stress can make a person forgetful.

If possible, have zero contact with the ex. If you must have contact, learn the gray rock strategy of not getting emotional and having pat, sound bite answers. Exercise, volunteer and stay busy. Life is too short to waste another second. Get going!

Dr. Pat: What did you do to heal?

Renee: It's quite a list. I stayed in therapy with you, Pat, and I was part of this support group where I got wonderful support even after the legal part of the divorce ended. Thank you all so much!

I hired a good lawyer. She told me the exact steps we'd follow and what I needed to do. She also told me flat out what to expect. My lawyer said divorce doesn't fix your life; it just ends the legal marriage.

I was a basket case when I first came to you for therapy, which you called PTSD. I had EMDR treatments that helped a lot. It took the sting out of some traumatic episodes.

I also went to Al Anon for a year to get even more support. I went for walks. I was broke financially and that was all I could afford to do. Healing has taken a long time, but I was in a diseased marriage for a long time.

I tried hard not to be angry or sad and to be happy for my kids. I didn't want to celebrate Christmas or anything the first year, but a friend said I had to, for the kids. So, there was some "fake it 'til you make it" going on. I did volunteer work, and still do. It helped me from obsessing about my own problems.

I felt so stupid about falling for his lies. I was embarrassed and ashamed. It took time to get over the anger at myself. I'm mostly there. Also, I apologized to my kids.

Dr. Pat: You were grieving the loss of the marriage you thought you had. And you were not stupid. Your ex was an expert at his craft.

Dr. Pat's Notes

- Allow yourself to feel the sadness or anger that comes with regret, then try to move toward broader thinking and less self-blame.

- Focusing on healing thoughts about all the things you did right will help you move into a better life.
- A great book by Daniel Pink is *The Power of Regret: How Looking Backward Moves Us Forward.*
- From Renee: Pay attention to what friends and family say about your boyfriend.
- From Renee: People say always have hope, but for me, hope was a noose that almost destroyed me. All I did was cope and hope. If you're in a bad relationship, stop hoping and get individual counseling. You can try marriage counseling also, but my ex was incredibly manipulative in couples counseling.
- Consult a lawyer to learn your options. Set up a bank account of your own. Have a safety plan in place and gather copies or originals of all your important documents. Take notes or keep a journal of your thoughts—in a notebook, not on your computer. You may need this later.

DEBBIE

Debbie: I'm just a bit younger than you, Renee, and I too had high hopes and dreams for life with my true love. Alcoholism and his cheating robbed me and my children of a loving family and destroyed our business. I came to view him and his bank buddies as thieves.

His lawyer accepted everything he said as the truth and even helped him lie in court. I felt angry and bitter for a while, but now I pity my ex. I forgave him for what he did to me. My faith demands that I forgive him, but it's harder when I think of my daughters. They are collateral damage. It still breaks my heart to know they don't have a loving father in their lives. But I'd marry him again if that was the only way I could have my girls.

Dr. Pat: Many women say their children were the only good thing they got out of their horrible marriages.

Debbie: I think so, yes. I was fooled and foolish, but I try to be a good person. As for advice I'd give to others—get out! I hung in there way too long with him. I wish I'd wised up earlier and acted on my "unease." Instead, I kept believing his lies.

Had I acted sooner to divorce him, we could've sold the business before he destroyed it, while it still had value. Then I wouldn't have struggled financially.

Dr. Pat: I want to take a moment here and talk about forgiveness. First, you never need to forgive the abuser. I repeat, you never need to forgive the abuser for the emotional and physical violence. But for your health and well-being you need to forgive yourself. If you continue blaming yourself for the dysfunction in your marriage, in a way you continue to abuse yourself. So please, dump the self – blame! You did not cause this abuse. When you forgive yourself, you begin to recover your self-respect; you begin to celebrate your survival; you begin to value your thoughts and feelings.

Debbie: Thanks, Pat. I need to keep working on forgiving myself. Something else I think is essential in a divorce is finding a good lawyer. I got through the divorce by finally giving up on getting anything from the business. I feel humbled by life and now realize I can't fix everything. I found solace in my faith—not the institution, but with the good people of my congregation. I joined a faith discussion group at my church, and we also do volunteer work. I think getting away from my own troubles and thinking of others helped me heal.

Dr. Pat: That's right. Doing volunteer work helps you feel like a productive member of society and keeps you from obsessing about your own problems.

Debbie: A friend of mine is going through a divorce now. She called to ask ME for advice. I guess I'm now a divorce expert! I told her to figure out the three most important things she absolutely needed to get out of it. My mistake was getting caught up in a million details that left me feeling overwhelmed. Had I been clearer and more focused from the start, I might have made out better and cut my losses.

Dr. Pat: What advice do you have for other women who are divorcing a narcissist?

Debbie: My parting advice is to talk to someone who has gone through a divorce. Disconnect from unhealthy people. Find your center every morning by mindful breathing and affirmative thoughts. I taped positive affirmation statements on yellow sticky notes all over my bathroom mirror. That's how I start my day.

Dr. Pat's Notes

- From Debbie: I hung in there way too long with him. I wish I'd wised up earlier and acted on my "unease." Instead, I kept believing his lies. Had I acted sooner to divorce him, we could've sold the business before he destroyed it, while it still had value. Then I wouldn't have struggled financially.
- Finding a good lawyer is essential!
- Doing volunteer work can help you feel like a productive member of society and keep you from obsessing about your own problems.

SHARON

Sharon: I think I told the group years ago that my ex's sister took me out to lunch before the wedding. She talked about their family life and said my fiancé had violent outbursts when he was younger. I told her he wasn't like that anymore—he was a brilliant, caring man, and I couldn't wait to marry him. I thought she was out of line for telling me this.

She tried to warn me and I ignored her. I missed other red flags as well. When we went out to eat, he did all the ordering. He'd often tell me what to wear. A couple of times he said I didn't know what I was talking about when I expressed an opinion about the economy or politics. Looking back, I see those were warning signs.

Dr. Pat: In hindsight you can see those red flags. Any other advice?

Sharon: I don't feel I should give advice after the mess I made of things. But if I could do it over, besides not marrying him, I know I stayed too long for the children. I thought I was helping them; I had no idea the impact my bad marriage was having on them. Now, I know they had a front row seat to their father insulting me while I struggled to cope. There was so much tension in our home. I was always trying to hide my tears. I don't know if they were aware of the violence.

Dr. Pat: If they didn't see it, they likely heard it. Children often have a gut sense of what's going on. It's hard to hide an unhappy, abusive marriage from them.

Sharon: When I saw my ex wrap his body around my son when he was little, saying that was just his way of hugging, I became concerned. Then I became alarmed. But I thought if I left him, we'd have a huge battle over the kids and I wouldn't be able to protect them. We did have a battle and I'm still fighting all these years later, but I now have full custody.

Dr. Pat: Many women stay in destructive marriages thinking it's best for the children. While the children will definitely need to make adjustments following the divorce, I believe it's always better to get out of an emotionally or physically abusive relationship. In the long run the children learn from your decision to leave an abuser. They learn to be strong and respect you for your decision. You rebuild a new family with you and the children.

If the children have contact with their father after the divorce, your job is to ensure they're safe with him, both emotionally and physically. If you don't think they're safe, then you need to do as Sharon did and try for full custody. I often recommend children get into therapy to help with the divorce transition, as well as to have their own advocate if need be.

Sharon, what words of advice do you have for other women?

Sharon: Never give up. The woman in the mirror can conquer anything because she's been to hell and back and no one will ever control her again. Keeping a healthy balance between work and kids saved me, and a job gave back my self-worth.

Dr. Pat: What did you do to heal?

Sharon: I let the ex take most of the furniture. I didn't argue over anything. I kept one set of everyday dishes and a couple of pots and pans. I told myself, "Good riddance!" to the furnishings in a house of misery and bought new furniture from a discount store. My mom helped a lot. I think the ex was surprised and probably angry that I wouldn't argue over objects. Cleaning out his stuff also helped me clear out my mind.

For anyone going through a divorce, I advise you not to fight over objects. I focused on my kids who were still young. I tried so hard to be a good mom. Life was calmer at home, for sure. Don't laugh, but I bought a book of jokes so I could tell them a joke every morning. That became a thing in our house. I stayed involved with their school and activities. I volunteered for every event.

I didn't go out much, but I read a lot of books and tried to get healthy and make good dinners. I have a tennis buddy—a girlfriend. I couldn't and wouldn't go to the club my ex frequents. I'm perfectly happy to play on the public tennis courts. Exercise is important because it makes me feel better.

I met a nice guy and we spent time together, but he died! I told you about him. That was awful. I recently started dating a man who is kind and respectful to me. And last year I got a job I love.

Whew! I feel like a new person, or maybe I'm getting back to the person I was before I met the ex.

Dr. Pat: That's right. You are recovering yourself!

Dr. Pat's Notes

- Try not to ignore red flag warnings from friends and relatives—and red flags in the relationship before you marry someone. That includes overbearing behavior, lying, bad temper, etc.
- From Sharon: I stayed too long for the children. I thought I was helping them; I had no idea the impact my bad marriage was having on them. Now, I know they had a front row seat to their father insulting me while I struggled to cope.
- Staying in an abusive marriage for the children is never a good idea. Children often have a gut sense of what's going on. It's hard to hide an unhappy, abusive marriage from them. In the long run, they learn to be strong and respect you for your decision to divorce.
- If the children have contact with their father after the divorce, your job is to ensure they're safe with him, both emotionally and physically. I often recommend children get therapy to help with the divorce transition.

- Rather than squabbling over objects, such as furniture, it's often better to say, "Good riddance!" and start your new life with a clean slate.

STEPHANIE

Dr. Pat: Stephanie, what can you share?

Stephanie: I spent my marriage blaming myself. I don't anymore. Like the others, I fell for an exciting and passionate man who made me laugh. When things went wrong, I tried to figure out how to fix them. I'm a fixer. And I kept hoping for happier days. I didn't realize I could never fix him because he was toxic.

He did a lot of bad things to me. I HAD to get out, and my family and my best friend told me over and over I should get a divorce, but I kept delaying. Like Renee, I thought hope was a good thing. Now I see that I was scared. I knew leaving would make him angrier. But I finally did it.

My sons were at home through all of it and experienced the arguments—him calling me a stupid bitch and him shoving me around. My ex brought out the worst in me. I yelled back and he'd storm out of the house.

I was a coward for taking so long to separate and file for divorce. I was kind of paralyzed with fear and confusion. As soon as he wasn't in the house anymore, there was quiet. I was able to finally think clearly. Pat, you helped me see what was going on. Staying in a horrible marriage was not good for my kids or me. I felt worthless, but you said ending the marriage was worth it.

Dr. Pat: YOU are so worth it! What advice would you give to others who are in a bad relationship?

Stephanie: If you're in a bad marriage, seek help! You are probably confused, exhausted and you can't see what's going on. It won't get better and will likely get worse. He could have killed me. My sons were teenagers who saw all of that, and now I have a son who's like a mini version of my ex. My son even calls me a stupid bitch like my ex did. I don't care about not having a husband, but I'm crushed that my son is an alcoholic and abusive to me and his girlfriend. I can't believe I have to go back to court to get the alimony my ex owes me. But I'm much stronger now.

Dr. Pat: You certainly are! He was counting on you to give up about the alimony, which would show he still has power over you. But you're standing up for yourself. Make sure your lawyer asks for a renewal of any protective orders. If the judge orders him to pay back alimony, he may act out.

Narcissistic sociopaths react badly when things don't go their way. I know you don't want to do this, but please also talk to your lawyer about options for getting a protective order from your son. It's drastic, but you may need it.

Stephanie, do you want to share any other wisdom?

Stephanie: Yes. Keep a positive attitude, exercise, get into a support group, and don't listen to toxic people. Get a job that gives you self-confidence. And, most importantly, make sure child support and alimony are wage garnished so you don't have to keep going back to court like I continue doing because my ex won't pay me what was court ordered.

Dr. Pat: Each of you look back on how you were fooled by your ex. After all, you're supposed to trust your husbands. You were angry at how you were treated and rightfully so. You used your anger as fuel to get out of a toxic relationship. It seems to me each of you realized you are worthy of having a sane life. You all had that moment of clarity when you realized you deserved better! As time passed, you began to detach from your ex and his abusive power and control.

You continued moving forward to build YOUR OWN LIVES. Why don't we use our next session to talk about how your lives have changed for the better and focus on the positive aspects of leaving an abusive relationship?

Dr. Pat's Notes

- Each of you are brave women and realized you are worthy of having a sane life. You each had that moment of clarity when you realized you deserve better.
- Hope is usually a positive thing, but it can keep you trapped in an abusive marriage. If you're in a bad marriage, seek help! You are probably confused, exhausted and you can't see what's going on. It won't get better and will likely get worse.
- Use your anger as fuel to release yourself from a toxic relationship.
- Narcissistic sociopaths react badly when things don't go their way. Stand up for yourself through your attorney. Make sure he pays alimony, obeys protective orders, and follows court mandated rules. As time passes, you will detach from your ex and his abusive power and control.
- Don't hesitate to seek a protective order if you feel threatened.

Discussion of Healing

Let Go or Be Dragged –Zen Proverb

Renee: There are lots of podcasts, shows, articles and books about healing. I even found a class at my old gym called Healing Yoga.

Dr. Pat: You don't go to the gym anymore?

Renee: Now I do stretching exercises every morning at home and I walk the dog every day. It works for me.

Dr. Pat: Okay. Just checking that you're getting some kind of physical exercise! What is your question about healing?

Renee: I'm having trouble even forming one question, but it seems to me that healing is going to be different for different people. Is there even a point when I can say "I am healed – Ta Da!" What is healing anyway?

Dr. Pat: Those are good questions. We talk about healing like everyone has the same understanding of it, but I agree that's not the case. Healing truly is different for different people—not one size fits all.

Let's talk about it. Debbie, what is your sense of healing or being healed for you?

Debbie: Well, I have no idea. Is healing just feeling okay? I can feel okay one day, and not okay the next day. I have monkey brain. Thoughts race around my head no matter what's going on in my life.

Dr. Pat: Can you see progress through the years after your separation and divorce?

Debbie: Oh, yeah! Before, during, and even for a couple of years after the divorce, I would go to bed at night and not be able to fall asleep. I kept thinking about all the things I should have done differently. The list was long. So at least part of healing for me means thinking about things *other* than what I should have done about my ex and our business. That change came slowly, but now, I seldom think these thoughts when I go to bed. I worry about other things!

Dr. Pat: Worry seems to be in your DNA, but letting go of that part of your past is a huge step forward. You have your children, friends, and your church work that are your primary concerns now, and, I hope, your joys, too.

Debbie: Definitely. I think about doing fun things with my friends, and I plan events at the church. I did the dating scene for a while, as I said earlier, and I still make craft jewelry at home. I took a trip to visit an old college friend across country I hadn't seen in ages. Traveling felt good. Actually, being contacted by Renee to get together again with The Group got my bad monkey brain going again.

Renee: Sorry.

Dr. Pat: Debbie, when you think about your marriage, divorce, and life after divorce, do you now think about them differently?

Debbie: Absolutely!

Dr. Pat: Is that difference a type of healing?

Debbie: Yes, now that I think about it, it is healing. Thoughts about my ex no longer hijack my brain or make me crazy. I can put those thoughts aside. I can sleep.

Dr. Pat: That is an important aspect of healing for you. Your past is always your past, but how you think about it—and when you think about it—changes dramatically as you "heal" from its wounds. What are your thoughts about healing, Stephanie?

Stephanie: I've got some monkey brain too, but for me, mornings were the problem. Before the divorce my morning thoughts were how to make the day as perfect as possible for him. Then it became how to survive each day. Then, I only thought about how to get through each day of the divorce, and try *not* to think about how blank the future felt.

I had no clue, and that was scary. So, I taped notes of positive sayings to the mirror in my bathroom and read them every morning. It helped to stop the morning monkey brain of doom and gloom. Whenever I came across a new quote I liked, I wrote it down and taped it on the bathroom mirror so I could read it in the morning.

Dr. Pat: What are your morning thoughts now?

Stephanie: Probably what normal people think about—what's going on at work today, any appointments, my grocery list, who I should call or text, why is my hair being weird. And I still add new positive notes whenever I see a good one.

Dr. Pat: You're quite normal, Stephanie! And keeping these positive affirmations front and center as you start each day is a healthy practice you can keep doing for your whole life. I'll suggest this to some of my other clients. Sharon, what does healing mean to you?

Sharon: I agree that healing is in your head. For me, it's also in my body.

Dr. Pat: Please explain.

Sharon: As my marriage deteriorated and I feared for the safety of myself and my kids, I became a person who lived mostly in the present. I was in survival mode, so I thought all day, every day, about things I needed to do, just to get by. My strategies had to keep changing depending on his mood and whether he was home or away on a business trip. I used to have my own work and interests, but that stopped after my marriage. Then the abuse escalated and got physical. It took everything I had to finally figure out how to get out.

Dr. Pat: As you all know, being in an abusive relationship is all-consuming. What about now?

Sharon: My ex intrudes every day with his drive-bys and texts, so there is no time of not thinking about him. But the impact of his behavior is a smaller part of my thoughts. He's like a barking dog on a leash. He would love to attack, but he can't. After I was awarded custody of the kids, and since I got a job, I'm less absorbed in thinking about strategies every minute. My thoughts are about my kids, my mom, my friends, and my new job. I actually read a couple of books last year! I care now about events and elections in my community.

Dr. Pat: Good for you!

Sharon: I also want to say again how important exercise is for me.

Dr. Pat: Yes, please tell us.

Sharon: I'm a health nut like I said. I hike, ski, and play tennis. During the worst years I pretty much stopped exercising. A friend had to drag me out a few times. I think lack of exercise kept me in a thinking funk also, if that makes any sense. Anyway, I'm playing tennis again twice a week and I go on hikes with my new friend.

Dr. Pat: You intuitively realize the mind-body connection, Sharon. Your ex also put hands on you, and your body keeps score. You are restoring health to your body and making sure your primary thoughts are about family, friends, and the new life you're living. There is definitely a connection between exercise and expansive thinking; just think about the blood and oxygen circulating through your body and brain when you move around. That goes for everything from walking the dog to playing tennis—just do it!

Sharon, you're purposeful about exercising regularly, even with your ex refusing to comply with the judge's orders to restrict contact. This is a process for your body and your mind, and you are making progress.

Renee: Can I talk more about thinking?

Dr. Pat: Of course.

Renee: I'm asking because you may not agree with what I'm thinking.

Dr. Pat: Talk anyway.

Obstacles To Healing

Renee: There are obstacles to healing—right?

Dr. Pat: Right. We're focusing now on the time after separation and divorce, not the obstacles to leaving in the first place. There are many obstacles in leaving an abusive relationship, and you've lived through them. You still face lots of obstacles after leaving, and that depends on what aspect of healing you're working on.

Stephanie: Money has been a big obstacle for me. I'm back in court for the alimony he owes me.

Dr. Pat: Money—before during, and after a divorce is almost always an obstacle during the healing process. You may worry about being poorer. But I have NEVER met a woman who would trade her former life of emotional or physical abuse for having better clothes or a nicer house.

Financial healing can mean eventually becoming financially independent. That may come in stages, because alimony and child support keep you connected to your ex for a period of time. Stephanie and Sharon are still tethered to their exes through financial ropes. Steph, you're hoping for a good outcome in your court hearing for the alimony he owes you. But you'll have to live with the decision.

Sharon, I'm sure you're counting the days until child support ends. You will have less money, but also, he won't have an excuse to contact you.

In general, I advise clients to figure out what's within their own control: can you downsize, get a job, or find a better paying job? Can you scale down expenses like entertainment, haircuts, groceries, or even share an apartment or house for the time being? Each of you did what you had to do. The overall advice for healing is to adjust to your current situation.

Debbie: I have a friend getting a divorce. She needs to see a therapist but can't seem to find a good one. She will get the divorce, but I worry that she'll still be a wreck.

Dr. Pat: In our country, we have obstacles to mental health care. Most of us need help with emotional and psychological healing after a divorce or for other reasons, but many people are blocked by cost, lack of insurance or a long waiting list. For some, it's transportation—can you physically get to a therapist or is online therapy an option? I hope this book gives more people access to a path for self-help healing.

People may also encounter obstacles to physical healing and getting medical care: cost, insurance, transportation, language, and cultural barriers. Then, moving forward, are you able to take the steps needed to eat healthy foods and get fresh air and exercise?

All of you had to overcome obstacles at every turn. You have been resourceful and persistent; you had to be.

Renee: Okay, but I've also been blocked from healing by something you said. You once said I enabled his abuse. I remember that session. I felt awful.

Dr. Pat: Please explain.

Renee: I thought of enabling as a kind of unintentional complicity. If I'd been more attuned to what was going on and been a stronger person, I could've nipped it in the bud. Although I don't think any conversation with him could have changed his behavior.

Dr. Pat: You're right about that.

Renee: Then, had I been smart enough and strong enough, I would've called a lawyer and filed for divorce after the first one or two mean things he said to me. If I hired a private investigator when he worked late and on weekends, I would've known early about his double life.

I used to view myself as a smart person. I was a good student and I went to college and grad school. I was a tax preparer, a job other people would tell me was hard, but it wasn't difficult for me. Even after all these years, thinking I enabled him is my greatest obstacle to feeling good about myself. I let a liar, a cheat and a creep take 27 years from me—and the operative word from an enabling point of view is—let.

I thought by always giving him another chance to do better and become a better person, I was being an optimist and even a good Christian. I thought those were good things. But I never, ever, had in my mind that I deserved his meanness, disrespect, or name calling.

Just because I didn't engage in open combat with him or walk out when he first started to be a jerk, I wasn't a meek mouse. At least, not in my head. I called him out in my own way—by walking away. I wouldn't listen to him. Sometimes, I'd tell him I disagreed with him. He would laugh or scoff. Then I stopped the conversation.

I don't think I ever yelled at him. That would've made things worse and accomplished nothing except exposing the kids to shouting. Outwardly, my silence or my seeming inaction may have looked like capitulation. I'm sure he thought that. But I was calculating. All the time.

Dr. Pat: Go on.

Renee: Once I realized I had to get out of the marriage, it became a matter of timing. And that took a while. When

I first thought of divorce, I was a stay-at-home mom with four children. Life went up and down for years. I kept recalculating the pros and cons. In *my* mind, I wasn't stupid. Yet in therapy, you told me I enabled his behavior. So, no matter what I do now, a footnote in my head reads: "And she enabled his abuse for 27 years." I actually played a role in my own abuse? I hate that label.

Dr. Pat: I'm sorry you've been struggling with this, Renee. I wish I'd known it was bothering you so we could talk it out. Just as everyone's healing is different, we may enable in different ways.

The term enabling came into existence around alcoholism. Often a codependent relationship develops between the alcoholic and the family. For example, if the alcoholic drinks to excess and can't make it into work because of a hangover, the spouse might call in for the husband with an excuse that he has the flu. Behavior like this allows alcoholics to not be accountable for their actions.

I imagine each of us can think of ways we enable someone in our lives. In an abusive relationship, enabling can take many forms. For example, you may excuse your spouse yelling at you because he had a rough day at work. Or you might excuse the fact that he doesn't help parent the children because his work is so important. The list can go on and on.

As you said Renee, this isn't done to protect the abuser—it's simply your rationale for tolerating his behavior and hoping it will get better. It is enabling if you don't speak up and say, "Hey, I need you to help more with the kids. Your parenting approach doesn't work for me. That isn't what I signed up for in marriage." Sometimes enabling behavior is silently tolerating irresponsible behavior.

When I say you enable, I'm not making you complicit in the abuse; I'm simply stating that you may be tolerating inexcusable behavior. Once you become aware that an abusive partner isn't going to change no matter what you do, then there may be an "aha" moment: "I've got to get out of this dysfunctional marriage."

Then the planful exit begins. You consult an attorney, you get a job, you go to therapy, you begin putting aside a nest egg of money. You carefully, and consciously, plan how you'll divorce this man. This often takes years, but you've stopped believing it will get better and begun to disengage, as best you can, from the abuser.

Again, it's important to understand that enabling does not cause the abuse. Enabling does not cause the drinking. Enabling does not cause the gambling. However, enabling does prevent you from looking at your own needs, while instead focusing on the needs of the other.

Again, you did not cause the abuse. And there's nothing wrong with having hope. But how long do you maintain that hope before you realize nothing will change in your abuser? What needs to change is your response to your abuser—which usually means finally having enough of his abuse and saying, "No more."

Please try to forgive yourself for whatever forms of enabling you may have done. We all enable in some ways. Things begin to change in our lives when we realize how and why we enable others.

Any Shortcuts?

Stephanie: Are there any shortcuts to healing? Or any ways to make the process go faster?

Dr. Pat: There is no definitive endpoint to healing, so there can't be a shortcut to that destination. Know that it is a process. The process itself *is* the healing, and your path will be different from another person's path. You all experienced unique incidents of trauma and accumulated trauma. The paths you choose will also be different.

Stephanie: It still feels so uncertain.

Dr. Pat: There was and is also only so much you can control. When we're young, we think we can control events. As we get older, we realize, not so much. For example, you all came to realize you couldn't fix your marriages.

Many things are beyond our control in life, and it's important to recognize that. You, Stephanie, have alimony owed to you, so you're still in the legal system. You also have a son who learned from his father to abuse you. You don't control the judge and you can't control or "fix" your son. Your current path will be different from Sharon's, who's ex contacts her every day to try and interfere with her life. Establishing and keeping boundaries are the hard challenges for each of you, but they take different forms. Debbie suddenly has both adult children back home with her. That's a new day-to-day life for her, however long it lasts. Renee is working on feeling good about herself.

Debbie: So how do you ever know you're on the right path?

Dr. Pat: Think about the progress you've made, Debbie. I wish we each had a formula to compute our progress—something like (New Experiences + Exercise + X = Happiness). But that isn't the case. You all feel better now than you did when we first met as a group, right? You all found a way. And you continue finding your own paths.

There was courage in the room when we first met and there is courage here today as you live your own lives. If I could extract anything from all your experiences, I think I'd say you have adjusted your expectations. You each had to grieve the "happier ever after marriage" you did not have. You let go of that fairy tale. You had to let it go. Because only then could you rebuild your lives slowly but surely, overcoming twists and turns and more than a few obstacles. You have adjusted your expectations.

You also have told me how grateful you are for what you have in your lives now—more sanity, quality time with friends and family, and the ability to make your own decisions—although each of you still have obstacles or rocks thrown at you from time to time. But you are stronger as you handle the rocks. You are stronger than you've ever been, and you've set good examples for your children and other people around you.

Debbie: My mom would say "What doesn't kill you, makes you stronger."

Renee: I guess so, but I could do without the almost getting killed part.

Stephanie: That reminds me of one of the quotes on my bathroom mirror: "There is a crack in everything. That's how the light gets in." It's also a magnet on my refrigerator, given to me by a friend who said I can use my broken pieces to let the light in. I guess it was a nice way of telling me I was in the dark about my marriage. I have seen the light!

Renee: I like that quote better. "There is a crack in everything. That's how the light gets in." Can I come to your house and read your bathroom mirror?

Debbie: That line is from a poem by Leonard Cohen and used on many positivity websites. Whose life doesn't have cracks?

Dr. Pat: Precisely. We all do. Life bruises us all. And you all have dealt with an awful lot. We've already talked about how it takes a toll on your minds and bodies. This quote is a positive way of thinking about light shining in the places where you have had emotional and physical injuries. As Renee said, it flips the script on looking at the broken or cracked places as more than just broken and cracked places. Instead, the broken and cracked places are openings to beautiful light. Light as warmth. Light as wisdom. It makes me think about repairing pottery.

Sharon: That's a leap!

Dr. Pat: Stay with me. I learned about this from a client once. In our western culture, we try to repair a broken vase, a bowl, or a mug so it's as good as new. If you can see the repair, we likely toss it out or put it in a garage sale.

Renee: Or we don't even try to fix it.

Dr. Pat: Exactly. We usually want things to be perfect or not at all. But in Japanese pottery there's a tradition to repair broken pieces using a shiny lacquer mixed with gold or silver so it highlights the damage rather than hiding it. This celebrates the story of the bowl or the vase—that it was once broken but is still lovely and useful. The imperfections actually make it more interesting. The Japanese method reframes brokenness as beauty and resilience.

Debbie: I just found this photo of Japanese broken pottery online. It's called Kintsugi.

Sharon: Wow. That is lovely!

Stephanie: Thanks for looking it up. I've never seen the quote as a picture.

Dr. Pat: Renee, why are you crying?

Renee: Because the broken bowl is so beautiful. I never looked at my broken-ness as having the potential for beauty. Now I can. Thank you!

Dr. Pat: I agree that it's beautiful. But it's no longer broken; it's stronger than ever, and so are each of you. Out of your broken parts you found the light and the courage to put back the pieces and make yourselves even better than before.

God will not look you over for your medals, degrees, or diplomas, but for your scars –Elbert Hubbard

Dr. Pat's Notes

Healing is a process that's always uneven and it is different for each of us. The ultimate goal is to shrink the hold the past abuse has on our present so we can be healthy in mind, body and soul, and enjoy our present and future lives.

Looking Forward

F.E.A.R. has two meanings – Forget Everything And Run Or Face Everything And Rise. The choice is yours. –Unknown

Dr. Pat: Each of you had coping strategies that were not only unhealthy, but dug you deeper into dysfunctional marriages. During that time, you lost yourselves, becoming fearful, angry, and tense. The relationships with your husbands brought out the worst in you.

Now, you're leading saner, happier, and safer lives. Through physical distance and the passage of time, each of you is recovering from years of toxicity, mostly through your own efforts to heal your bodies and minds. This is a process. Thank you for sharing your hard-earned wisdom with others through this book.

Now let's look into the future. What do you see when you look forward?

Renee: What an interesting question! Before the divorce I lived in the moment, just coping one hour at a time. I barely thought about the future. During the divorce, I felt like I was standing on the edge of a cliff, looking into darkness. I didn't have a clue about the future or how I'd survive.

Now, more than ten years after the divorce, I'm free to look forward. I'm the oldest here, but I feel kind of new, like I have a new lease on life. I will continue to cherish my kids—all grown now—and fill my life with what I love: family and friends, including new friends; gardening; learning to cook new recipes; volunteer work; and my alone time with my books. I can't afford to travel, but books are a wonderful escape from the mundane. Come to think of it, I'm grateful for the mundane, because feeling calm every day is a gift. I have time to think.

Debbie: I agree! I value calm days. I'm also deep into volunteer work with my congregation, which makes me feel alive and useful. I had to release a lot of anger about my marriage and bitterness about losing the business. But after releasing those feelings I felt lighter, even though I've put on a few pounds!

I know I don't *need* a man in my life, and dating is no longer a goal for me. Loving my kids and giving back to my community are my priorities. I'm glad and grateful I have more years ahead.

Stephanie: Right now, I'm struggling to think beyond my legal problems, because I'm trying to recover alimony my ex hasn't paid. But I know I'll have a life of my own, whatever the outcome.

I don't know if I'll ever have a good relationship with my son Evan. I realize I can't fix him, but I'll always love him and his brother.

I make a point of keeping in touch with friends and new acquaintances. I will keep my boundaries with my boyfriend. He knows where I stand: No marriage in the future. I'm closer to my sister than ever and we're planning a vacation together when we can afford it. I can dream, can't I?

Sharon: It seems strange that I can be happy now, after being miserable for so many years. I have a new job, a couple of good friends, a nice boyfriend, and I treasure my kids and my mom. I can focus on these things.

I do not let my ex invade my mind, although he keeps trying to mess with my head all the time. I count my blessings, and when I look in the mirror, I see a strong woman, not a victim. But recovery takes time and I know I need to continue working on it. I hope to keep getting stronger and healthier, and be an example to my kids.

Dr. Pat: Maya Angelou, a wise woman, once said: "When you know better, you do better." You all know so much more now, and you are doing much, much better!

How do I Feel Now?

I sleep alone soundly.
I cook for one simply.
I love my kids wholly.
I plant my garden contentedly.
I listen to my mind quietly.
I wear the clothes I choose.
I go for walks when I choose.
I clean my house as I choose.
I watch what I choose and I read what I want.
I am poorer but more worthwhile,
rich in calm and sanity.
Untethered to the past and much lighter.
Being okay is now more than okay.
I am facing forward.

by Renee Forte

PART III: THINGS YOU NEED TO KNOW

"Hope is a woman who has lost her fear." –Alice Walker

Post Separation Power and Control

Abusers will continue sowing chaos after a relationship ends due to their need to maintain **Power and Control.** A narcissistic sociopath may use any means possible to hang onto control—often through the children, child support payments and alimony. In fact, power and control are often illustrated as the center of a wheel around which the various types of abuse rotate. Courts, law enforcement and the former non-abusing partner need to recognize these patterns and try to guard against them.

Post Separation Abuse may include these types described at: www.domesticshelters.org:

Legal Abuse: The abuser continues to use court proceedings and false reports of child abuse to try to control, harass, and impoverish the other parent.

Harassment, Monitoring, Stalking: The abuser continuously calls their ex or sends emails, texts, and instant messages. These messages may concern child-related matters, but their true intention is to interfere as much as possible with the ex-partner's ability to live a peaceful life. The monitoring may even include apps or devices that track or record their ex-partner's activities and communication. The abuser may frequently drive past the house or workplace, or show up at events just to provoke anxiety and fear in the other parent.

Threats: The abuser may give outright threats of bodily or economic harm, or say "Remember, I have a gun," or "What if something happens to you, God forbid?" Abusers sometime threaten to release sexual images to ruin their ex's reputation and livelihood. Or they threaten to block the ex-partner from ever seeing the children. Unfortunately, abusers sometimes carry out these threats.

Isolation: The abuser may try to discredit the former partner, spreading rumors among friends, family, co-workers, congregations, physicians, therapists and even their children's teachers to make the other parent look bad or deprive their former partner of a support system.

Counter-Parenting. The abuser works against, rather than with, the other parent. Those engaged in counter-parenting will undermine the protective parent's rules, such as efforts to have children complete their schoolwork or to go to bed at a certain time. They will complicate the exchange of possessions, like losing items. In the transitions from one parent to the other, there will be delays in pick-up or drop-off, or they make sudden changes in the schedule. Counter-parenting also includes making phone calls as tense as possible, rather than promoting harmony.

Neglectful or Abusive Co-Parenting: The abuser may try to avoid blatantly abusing their children, but will fail to protect the child adequately, engage in risky behavior, or engage in outright neglect. Other abusers will physically, psychologically or sexually abuse their children as a way to get back at their ex-partner.

Abuse by Proxy: The abuser, post separation, tries to weaponize the children and use them as pawns to torment the former spouse. They may degrade the former partner to their children, accuse her of things she didn't do, or make the children fear her. All this is an attempt to get the children to reject, avoid or act aggressively toward the other parent. They will also use the children to undermine the no contact order.

Economic Abuse. The abuser fails to follow through on needed support, even with court ordered payments. The abuser might even go so far as stealing the former partner's identity to take out loans in her name and try to wreck her credit. The abuser can also do seemingly petty but costly actions, such as signing a child up for activities without paying the fee, so the other parent has to pay these unexpected fees or disappoint the child. Or the abuser loses items of clothing, so the former partner is forced to buy multiple jackets, clothes, or shoes. Abusers often quit or choose to "lose" their job rather than pay support to the other parent of their children, sometimes rendering that parent and the children destitute and homeless in the process.

Sexual Abuse. Some abusers continue to coerce their ex-partners, using forced sex as a condition of keeping the children safe.

Safety Advice

For your safety

The first year after leaving an abusive relationship is the most dangerous time for you. The abuser may act on impulse to regain control and power. The Department of Justice documented that 75% of domestic assaults reported to law enforcement agencies were inflicted *after* the couple separated.

- Don't ignore threats. Call the police if you feel threatened in any way.
- Request a permanent protective order as part of your legal proceedings; let law enforcement know of your protective order.
- If your community allows it, file for a no trespass order with the police. Try to make an alliance with at least one police officer and with local domestic violence police units.
- Change all locks on your doors and install electronic door monitoring. Install a safety camera and security

system in the house. Have motion sensitive outside lights installed.

- Let some of your neighbors and your workplace know about your safety concerns.
- Block his calls and change your email address. Have the family phones and computers checked to make sure he isn't tracking and monitoring you and the children.
- Create a safety escape plan in case the abuser should enter your home. Keep car keys, money, and cell phone in a convenient place to grab when exiting. Some women have go-bags ready for themselves and the children.
- Have a safe house or houses you can go to, plus people you can call if you need to flee quickly at any time, day or night. Check if your community has a women's shelter, in case you need it overnight.
- Make safety plans in your workplace, as well. Inform security officers and coworkers of your situation and show them a photo of your abuser.
- Call the police each time there is a trespass or threat. You are building a record of the danger or non-compliance with the court's orders.

For your children

- Ask the court to order the use of the Our Family Wizard (OFW) app or another app as the only means of communication—and stick to it.
- Let your children's schools, coaches, doctors, and the parents of their friends know about the situation.
- Ask the court to order continuing therapy for your children.
- With the advice of a lawyer, make a will naming a person you trust as guardian of your minor children.
- Domestic shelters give this advice to address difficult behavior from your children: "Try to remember this isn't personal. Children are often following an abuser's direct or indirect orders. The abuser is working hard to undermine and diminish your role as the protective parent. You may be tempted to punish your children or cut them off because of how they treat you. Healing begins when you can regulate your own behavior and move from reactive to responsive, creating a feeling of safety for your child. Take a breath before you respond in anger or defensiveness." (www.domesticshelters.org)

- Seek family counseling for you and the children together. This can help get to the bottom of issues and provide documentation if you file for full custody or a restraining order.
- Document violations of the court orders, and file for full custody if necessary to protect the children.

Financial

- Push hard for garnishment of his wages to pay child support and alimony.
- Freeze your credit through the credit reporting agencies. Open new accounts in your name alone.
- Make sure any deeds of transfer are completed when the lawyers are involved. Protect your home with a homestead declaration if possible.
- Be sure to change the beneficiary of your pension and insurance policies.

General Safety Advice

- Cut -off or minimize all contact and communication with the toxic former spouse and probably also their family and friends.

- Remember, *you* have changed; you want a sane, safe and calm family life. Your abuser has not changed. While no contact isn't possible when children are involved, limit your communication and confine it to what the court ordered.
- Practice being a **gray rock** to shut down efforts to expand contact. Your children will come to see you as safe and sane as you all recover from the divorce.

Recovery Toolkit

To help re-build the New You, we've have put together a toolkit to assist with recovery and healing. Remember, you've been through years of abuse and it may take years to completely recover.

Please be patient with yourself. Begin and end each day with a pat on the back and a hug for having the courage and fortitude to leave the abuse behind. You've been through a battle, and it takes time to heal and recover. You can begin by taking one small step each day.

Wellness is more than being free from illness; it's a dynamic process of change and growth. It means becoming aware of where we are emotionally, physically, and spiritually, then making choices that lead to a healthy and fulfilling life.

Wellness is composed of eight vital dimensions:

- social,
- emotional,
- spiritual,
- occupational,
- intellectual,
- creative,
- financial
- and physical.

This section shows a variety of ways to move toward holistic wellness in all eight dimensions.

Stress management

Recognizing when you're stressed is an important first step. Perhaps you've lived with stress for so long that you don't even know what life feels like without it. Releasing your stress and the "fight or flight" attitude may feel dangerous at first. Occasional stress is normal for everyone, but you've probably lived this way for years. The good news—you can change!

Separation and divorce may create a different set of stressful situations, but now YOU are in control. Taking one thing at a time and learning to manage your stress will help you build the new, happier life you deserve.

Recognize your signs of stress

Physical: Do you have back pain, headaches, muscle tension, changes in appetite, sleep disturbance, rapid heartbeat or breathing?

Emotional: Are you irritable, sad, angry, afraid, depressed, moody, hopeless, powerless, helpless? Do you have anxiety attacks?

Cognitive: Do you have difficulty concentrating, trouble remembering things, feel confused, catastrophize, feel doubt, have perfectionistic tendencies?

Behavioral: Do you overwork, snap at others, feel impulsive, pace the floor, withdraw, have poor self-care, use drugs or alcohol more than usual, have increased conflicts, irritability, nightmares, elevated startle response, hypervigilance?

Spiritual: Do you feel a loss of purpose, pervasive helplessness, anger and/or questioning of prior religious beliefs, anger at God or higher power?

Interpersonal: Are you withdrawing from family and friends, showing decreased interest in intimacy, mistrust and isolation from friends, and disinterest in parenting?

What positive techniques have already worked for you to relieve stress?

Perhaps you find relief with such things as reading, taking a walk, listening to music, working on puzzles, socializing, playing games on your smartphone, exercising, journaling, knitting, taking a relaxing bath, or having alone time (not isolating.)

Here are a few additional ways to handle stress in your life:

Try to eliminate stressors: While it isn't always possible to escape a stressful situation or avoid a problem, you can change how you react and respond. Evaluate how you can manage situations that cause stress by dropping some responsibility, relaxing your standards, or asking for help. You may need to step back from activities that take too much of your time and energy.

Rest/protect your sleep: Rest is crucial. Stress has taken a toll on your body and you've probably had issues with sleep. For restorative sleep, stop using your devices and computer right before bedtime. This has to do with the blue light emitted from electronic devices that activates your brain to think it's daytime and you need to be alert. Keep your devices away from your bed. A calming book or listening to music is much better.

Get exercise: Exercise is crucial. Brisk movement can improve your sleep and help you work off stress that lingers in your body. Regular walking is helpful. Gentle stretching each morning or yoga helps many people. For others, rigorous exercise is the goal—lifting weights, cycling, swimming, running marathons, or climbing mountains. Just don't be reckless!

Spend time in nature: Get out to a park or walk in a nature preserve. Forest Bathing is a technique of awareness using the sounds and sights of nature.

Rebuild your self-esteem: I often say the women I see in therapy who are in abusive relationships are like mighty oaks that have been whittled down over the years by abuse and constant belittling. They've become toothpicks of their former selves.

In time, with continued effort and self-improvement, you can become a strong rooted tree once again. You need to nurture yourself in order to grow again and become that healthy tree. Just as a tree will regrow itself from a tree trunk, the time has come to rebuild your new self.

For years you've been controlled and criticized by your abusive ex, so now you need to turn that negativity to positivity. Make a list of all your positive, wonderful qualities. For example, you might include:

- Professional skills (dedicated, skilled, hard worker, team player, on time, committed, etc.)
- People skills (thoughtful, good listener, giving, good communicator, etc.)
- Wonderful mother, daughter, sister, friend.
- Common sense and intelligence.
- Human values (honest, trustworthy, loyal, kind, etc.)
- Outlook (positive, fun loving, upbeat, sense of humor, etc.)
- Outlook related to world (volunteer, animal lover, environmentally aware, sustainability, social justice, etc.)
- Talents (creative, artistic, athletic, musical, good decorator, writer, actor, etc.).

Advice From Renee: Flip the script!

During my divorce and for a while afterward, I still focused on the past—what could have happened and should have happened. I felt stuck. I began researching positivity sites online and found a quote by author Maya Angelou that changed the way I think:

"What you're supposed to do when you don't like a thing is change it. If you can't change it, change the way you think about it."

My version of her wise advice is "flip the script." That means changing the message in my mind from negative to positive. For example, I kept thinking my life was over because I wasted so many years in a terrible marriage.

I stopped that script from replaying in my mind and took stock of where I was. Yes, I have many years behind me, but I'm still alive, with years ahead to love my friends and family and be a productive member of my community.

Another example is the date my granddaughter was born, which happened to be my wedding anniversary date—the one time in the entire year I did *not* want her to be born! But she had other ideas. That day was filled with joy at her birth and I came to see her birth as helping me flip the script for that date, from dread and regret, to joy and celebration for my granddaughter.

A final example is flipping the script away from feeling like a failure because you married a liar, cheat and creep, and stayed so long. I flipped that script in my head and now see myself as a strong woman who got out, financially poorer, but much richer in the parts of my life money can't buy. And I no longer answer to him about how I spend my money or how I "spend" my life. Woo hoo!

Forgive yourself: You most likely have regrets; we all do. One of your regrets is marrying your ex or having children with your ex. You love your children, but hate that he is their father. You may regret staying in the abusive relationship too long. These are all normal regrets for all women who leave abusive relationships.

Daniel Pink's book, *The Power of Regret: How Looking Backward Moves Us Forward*, addresses regrets as a healthy and necessary step for moving forward in a positive direction.

Pink says it's important to feel regret and talk about it, but we shouldn't get stuck in that dark place. When thinking about regret, it's helpful to distance yourself a bit and analyze how you want to move forward. He talks about the importance of self-compassion in moving forward.

View yourself as though you're another person—a friend who needs advice. You would certainly feel compassion for someone in a similar situation. Look at the compassion you feel for another and apply it to yourself.

You never need to forgive the abuser, but you do need to forgive yourself. As long as you continue blaming yourself for what happened in your marriage, the abuse continues because, in a way, you are abusing yourself. If you haven't been blaming yourself, then forgiveness isn't necessary.

Forgiving yourself is a celebration of your survival. By stopping the blame, you empower yourself to stand up to the abuse and begin recovering your self-respect. You begin to respect yourself—your insights, judgment, values, and perspective on the world.

Build New Experiences: Staying in a fetal position will keep you trapped in your thoughts reliving bad experiences. Get out of bed, off the couch, and do new things. You don't have to take an exotic trip, although you could. Volunteer somewhere, learn to knit, join a club, or get a new job. Or do old things as the "new you," like holidays and birthdays. Save some of your traditions, but also start new ones. Here, you may have to fake it 'til you make it, but stick with the process! As time passes, new experiences will take you further and further from your toxic relationship.

Keep your pleasurable activities: When we're stressed, we often drop out of leisure activities. It's important to keep doing things that please us. Even when time gets tight, please make a little time for yourself. Read a novel, sing along with a favorite tune, dance in your kitchen, stream your favorite comedy on TV, take a hot bath, get a manicure or pedicure, get a new haircut. Do something nice for yourself every day.

Monkey brain/obsessing: Become aware of negative self-talk. Cognitive therapy is about recognizing negative statements you may repeat to yourself, such as: "I can't make it on my own," "I'm not good enough at anything to survive," or "He's right, I am the problem."

These obsessive statements occur because you heard them in your abusive marriage. Now is the time to divorce yourself from false beliefs and damaging statements. When you have disturbing thoughts, redirect your brain to positive affirmations, such as:

- I am a powerful woman who has already done amazing things.
- I divorced a sociopath. That is no small task. I survived!
- I can, and WILL, rebuild and start a new life for myself and my children.

- It's my life now. I can make it however I want it to be. I am free.

In time the negative statements will be replaced by your positive, supportive affirmations. The Kripalu Center for Yoga and Health suggests the following methods to move beyond obsessive negative thoughts:

- Move your body! Get up and walk, do jumping jacks or a Youtube seven- minute workout.
- Get into nature. Go to a park, smell a rose, take a trail hike.
- Sing, dance, create.
- Connect with positive people.

Stay away from triggers: If a place, a restaurant, a song, former in-laws, and other triggers threaten to suck you back into a dreadful episode or pattern, avoid these situations, at least until they lose their sting. You are in charge now!

Eat healthy: While a carton of ice cream, a bag of potato chips, or a bottle of wine will bring short term pleasure, turn your focus to restoring your long-term health. You don't have to eat kale! But focus on eating fresh food when you can, knowing you're restoring your body to good health as you heal your physical and mental wounds.

Have fun: Fun is not just for kids. Let your inner child come forward. Remember childhood things that brought joy; remember the little girl who's still inside you. If you did not have a happy childhood, allow yourself to have that childhood now. Fly a kite, build a sandcastle, dance in the rain, splash in a puddle. HAVE FUN!

Choose positive, supportive people in your new life: After leaving an abusive relationship you need to re-evaluate the people in your life. Have they, too, been critical and negative voices in your head? Have they undermined you instead of offering encouragement? This is the time to take a good, long look at who deserves to remain in your inner circle. Don't take criticism from people you wouldn't ever go to for advice.

Join a support group for women who've been in abusive relationships. These women get it. They understand.

Spiritual wellness: Establishing peace, harmony, and balance is important as you seek meaning and purpose for your new life. Finding the spiritual part of yourself can accelerate and add joy to the healing process. Spiritual connection is a personal thing: For some people it includes religious-based faith, while others find solace with their own belief systems that may involve nature or meditating. Your spiritual journey is a personal decision, but no matter what path you choose, healing spiritually will help you feel more content and connected to life.

Seek help: If you still feel overwhelmed and self-help isn't enough, look for a psychologist or other mental health provider who can help you manage stress and deal with the changes in your life. Schedule individual visits with a therapist who's skilled in working with abusive relationships. Having this expert guidance can help you move into your new life and decide who you want to become.

My Therapist

You give a name to my feelings.

You let me cry.

I flit from topic to pain.

Can I give you this much awfulness?

"What else happened?" you say.

I read, watch, and listen to the news each day.

"What is your news?" you ask.

"What is your current event?"

This, that, and this.

What is happening to me, I ask?

Am I losing my mind: I am scared of tomorrow.

"You are on a current." You say.

When will it end?

I don't know," you say, "But it will end."

You name the pain. You sponge the pain.

You guide the boat through fierce white water.

"You can cry," you say. "It is good to cry.

Tears take your river to a new place."

By Renee Forte

Types of Therapy

When you're considering therapy, the closest women's shelter may be able to recommend local therapists who specialize in abusive relationships.

Cognitive behavior therapy is designed to help clients identify unhealthy negative thinking patterns. Replacing negative thoughts with more accurate, rational thoughts helps people break free of negative thinking, lessen anxiety, and begin to heal their emotions.

An **eclectic** therapist may use many different approaches to therapy, based on the needs of each client. Approaches to therapy include psychodynamic, interpersonal, humanistic, behavioral to name a few.[12] No matter which techniques they use, the most important element is finding a therapist who fits your needs and can create warmth, empathy, and rapport.

If you're dealing with intrusive thoughts related to the abusive relationship, **EMDR (eye movement desensitization reprocessing)** is a relatively new technique designed to help "rewire" the brain for clients dealing with trauma and

---

12 Jonathan Engel, *American Therapy: The Rise of Psychotherapy in the United States*. Gotham, 2009.

other distressing life experiences. This therapeutic technique requires a specialist in EMDR training and can be used with other types of psychotherapy.

S.E. (somatic experiencing) therapy is a growing practice which suggests the source of healing lies in the body rather than the mind. The basic idea behind somatic therapy originates in the research of Bessel van der Kolk and is described in his best-selling book, *The Body Keeps the Score*. This therapy must be provided by a trained, certified S.E. therapist.

Group therapy can be extremely helpful. Finding a support group of women who are now, or have been, in abusive relationships may be difficult, but worth the effort. The power of a supportive group changes people who may be stuck in individual therapy and dysfunctional relationships. Sharing our stories helps us feel less alone, less damaged. Every group's power comes from the willingness of each member to trust the group and share. In sharing stories, including the painful parts, each group member feels free to disclose her own difficulties.

The willingness to be vulnerable and share our flaws, weaknesses, and struggles, gives everyone in the group permission to reveal and be honest as well. As blogger and author Carol Christ wrote:

> When one woman puts her experiences into words, another woman who has kept silent, afraid of what others will think, can find validation. And when the second woman says aloud, "Yes, that was my experience too, the first woman loses some of her fear.

Post-Traumatic Growth: Envision Your Future in Five Years

Trauma is a fact of life. It does not, however, have to be a life sentence.–Peter A. Levine

The future can look bleak when you're struggling to recover from a relationship that threatened the very core of your being. However, in recent years, researchers and mental health professionals have embraced the concept of post-traumatic growth. It's all about rebuilding a better, stronger version of yourself.

The first step is a mindset shift: stop seeing yourself as a victim and begin realizing you can be a proud survivor and grow stronger every day, even as you make difficult decisions and face problems.

You can change the way you feel and behave by changing the way you think about yourself.

These 10 steps toward post-traumatic growth and regaining happiness are from the website https://www.happierhuman.com/post-traumatic-growth/:

- Embrace your painful emotions so that you may have the strength to overcome them
- Put aside the painful past and turn your attention towards the present
- Create a personal story in which you are the proud survivor
- Stick to a pleasant routine
- Allow yourself to receive the support of those who care about you
- Use meditation to gain some piece of mind
- Invest in new and exciting activities
- Be optimistic
- Place yourself first and care for your needs

- And lastly, be patient.

Trauma, no matter how painful and unbearable it might seem, presents a fantastic opportunity for growth. It's up to you to seize it and regain the happiness and joy of living.

Your Five-Year Plan

As you look forward to a better future, setting goals will help you see light at the end of the tunnel. Creating a five-year life plan leads you toward realizing how beautiful and fulfilling your life can be. These are a few areas to consider as you develop a plan for your future:

- Job or Career
- Education
- Friendships
- Intimate relationships
- Family life
- Health Goals
- Physical appearance

The first step is to consider your goals for each of the above categories. How would you like to see yourself a year from now? Then try to devise an action plan to achieve these goals.

For example,

Goal: Career – I would like to get a full-time job in the area of public relations

Plan: Career

1. Get help writing a great resume.

2. Explore job opportunities.

3. Determine if need more education or training.

4. Practice interviewing skills.

5. Interview and start work!

The following books explain and give examples of goal setting and creating action plans

- *Goal Setting: How to Create an Action Plan and Achieve Your Goals,* by Susan Wilson and Michael Dobson, Amacom, 2008.
- *Creating Your Best Life: The Ultimate Life List Guide,* by Caroline Adams and Michael Frisch, Union Square and Company, 2021.
- *Your Best Year Ever: A 5-Step Plan for Achieving Your Most Important Goals,* by Michael Hyatt, Baker Books, 2018.
- *The Art of Setting Smart Goals,* by Anisa Marku, 2019.
- *You Goal, Girl: A Goal-Setting Workbook,* by Melissa Bowles and Elise Rikard, Rock Point, 2018.

The Open Door

A door opens. Maybe I've been standing here shuffling my weight from foot to foot for decades, or maybe I only knocked once. In truth, it doesn't matter. A door opens and I walk through without a backward glance. This is it, then; one moment of truth in a lifetime of truth; a choice made, a path taken; the gravitational pull of Spirit too compelling to ignore any longer. I am received by something too vast to see. It has roots in antiquity but

Moving on from a Narcissist

speaks clearly in the present

tense. "Be," the vastness says.

"Be without adverbs, descriptors

or qualities. Be so alive that

awareness bares itself

uncloaked and unadorned.

Then, go forth to give what you

alone can give. Awake to love

and suffering, unburdened by

the weight of expectations.

Go forth to see and be seen,

blossoming, always blossoming

into your magnificence."

by Danna Faulds

In Closing

"One day you will tell the story of how you overcame what you went through, and it will be someone else's survival guide."–Amazingmemovement.com

"The most beautiful people we have known are those who have known defeat, known suffering, known struggle, known loss, and have found their way out of the depths.

These persons have an appreciation, a sensitivity, and an understanding of life that fills them with compassion, gentleness, and a deep loving concern. Beautiful people do not just happen." –Elizabeth Kubler-Ross

"You are not the darkness you endured. You are the light that refused to surrender." –John Mark Green

"Never let someone who contributes so little to a relationship control so much of it." –Anonymous

"I now see how owning our story and loving ourselves through that process is the bravest thing that we will ever do." –Brené Brown

"Each time a woman stands up for herself, without knowing it possibly, without claiming it, she stands up for all women." –Maya Angelou

"Survivor Psalm: I have been victimized. I was in a fight that was not a fair fight. I did not ask for the fight. I lost. There is no shame in losing such fights. I have reached the stage of survivor and am no longer a slave of victim status. I look back with sadness rather than hate. I look forward with hope rather than despair. I may never forget, but I need not constantly remember. I was a victim. I am a survivor."
–Unknown

RESOURCES

www.Apa.org (American Psychological Association) Resource for many mental health related topics including narcissistic disorder and sociopathic disorder, as well as domestic violence and PTSD.

www.emdria.org How to find a clinician for EMDR.

www.emdr.com Information on EMDR Institute: trainings, clinicians and description of EMDR.

https://traumahealing.org Information on Somatic Experiencing therapy: what it is and clinicians.

https://www.theembodylab.com Somatic Psychology and Trauma Recovery programs and training.

www.somaticexperiencing.com The Ergos Institute of Somatic Education with Peter Levine PhD.

amazingmemovement.com Site that shares positive and inspirational messages of hope inspired by real women's stories.

www.CoDA.org Recovery program for codependence: find a meeting and descriptions of codependence.

www.niaaa.nih.gov National Institute on Alcohol Abuse and Alcoholism. Treatment for alcohol problems: finding and getting help.

www.samhsa.gov Free, confidential, 24/7 treatment referral and information service for substance abuse and mental health services.

www.aa.org Alcoholics Anonymous: Resource to help find an AA meeting near you.

www.al-anon.org Al Anon: Resource to find an Al-Anon meeting near you.

www.al-anon-alateen-msp.org Al Ateen: Resource to find an Alateen meeting near you.

www.theduluthmodel.org A resource to help deepen the understanding of the tactics listed on the Duluth Model Power and Control wheel of domestic abuse. Includes information on trainings and therapy.

www.domesticshelters.org – A comprehensive website and easy to search database to identify types of abuse, strategies for leaving, finances, children, the courts, and how to find a shelter and connect with an advocate, and post separation abuse.

https://centerforhopewny.org Center for Hope WNY Resource for hope, help and healing from Narcissistic Abuse. Workshops, information, podcasts and webinars.

www.Stopabuseforeveryone.org SAFE provides educational information for victims of abuse and domestic violence, regardless of their gender, age, race, sexual orientation and beliefs.

www.cafemom.com/single-mom Resource for moms related to parenting, mental health, being a single mom.

www.singlemotherguide.com Information of benefits and places for single moms to get federal grants and assistance.

www.SPAOA.org Single Parents Alliance of America provides support and resources for housing, financial benefits and grants.

www.rainn.org Rape, Abuse and Incest National Network: Information on services offered to help victims of sexual abuse.

ASCA *Survivor to Thriver Manual Workbook for Adult Survivors of Child Abuse* and information on support meetings.

APPS for PC and Devices

Our Family Wizard App: An app designed to help reduce conflict after divorce related to co-parenting.

Bright Sky App: A free and easy to download mobile app providing support and information for anyone who may be in an abusive relationship or those concerned about someone they know.

BOOKS and ARTICLES:

The New York Times Magazine, May 21, 2023 "Should You Be in Therapy?"

Psychology Today blog: *www.psychologytoday.com/us/blog/invisible-chains/202208/7-commom-post-separation-abuse-tactics*

Domestic Abuse Tactics: *www.domesticshelters.org/articles/legal/8-common-post-separation-domestic-abuse-tactics*

Dugan, Meg and Hock, Roger. *It's My Life Now: Starting Over After an Abusive Relationship or Domestic Violence.* New York: Routledge, 2000.

Engle, Jonathan. *American Therapy: The Rise of Psychotherapy in the United States.* Gotham: 2009.

Faulds, Donna. *From Root to Bloom: Yoga Poems and Other Writings.* Greenville, VA: Peaceable Kingdom Books, 2006.

Gottman, John and Silver, Nan. *The Seven Principles for Making Marriage Work.* New York. Harmony books, 2015.

Kubler-Ross, Elisabeth. *Death, The Final Stage of Growth.* New York: Scribner, 1997.

Martin, Patricia and Forte, Renee. *Liars, Cheats, and Creeps: Leaving the Narcissist Behind.* Longmeadow, MA: PetersMartinPress, 2025.

Martin, Patricia and Houston, Helene. *The Patient Knows: Wisdom from The Other Couch.* Longmeadow, MA: PetersMartinPress, 2025.

Pink, Daniel H. *The Power of Regret: How Looking Backward Moves Us Forward.* New York: Riverhead Books, 2022.

Van Der Kolk, Bessel. *The Body Keeps the Score.* New York: Penguin Group, 2014.

Books on Goal Setting and Action Plans:

- *Goal Setting: How to Create an Action Plan and Achieve Your Goals,* by Susan Wilson and Michael Dobson, Amacom, 2008.
- *Creating Your Best Life: The Ultimate Life List Guide,* by Caroline Adams and Michael Frisch, Union Square and Company, 2021.
- *Your Best Year Ever: A 5-Step Plan for Achieving Your Most Important Goals,* by Michael Hyatt, Baker Books, 2018.
- *The Art of Setting Smart Goals,* by Anisa Marku, 2019.

- *You Goal, Girl: A Goal-Setting Workbook*, by Melissa Bowles and Elise Rikard, Rock Point, 2018.

HOTLINES:

National Domestic Violence Hotline 1- 800-799-7233 (SAFE) *www.ndvh.org*

National Dating Abuse Hotline 1 -866-331-9474

National Child Abuse Hotline/ Childhelp 1-800-4-A-CHLD 1 – 800 422-4453

National Sexual Assault Hotline 1- 800-273-8255 (TALK)

National Center for Victims of Crime 1-202-467-8700 *www.victimsofcrime.org*

National Human Trafficking Resource Center/ POLARIS Project 1-888-373-7888 or text HELP to BE FREE (233733) *www.polarisproject.org*

National Resource Center on Domestic Violence 1-800-537-2238 *www.nrcdv.org*

National Runaway Safeline 1-800-786-2929 1-8-RUNAWAY *www.1800runaway.org*

National Deaf Domestic Violence Hotline (NDDVH) 855-812-1001 (voice/VP) *www.thedeafhotline.org*

Woman of Color Network Hotline 1-800-537-2238 www.wocninc.org

About the Authors

Patricia Peters Martin, Ph.D., is a Phi Beta Kappa graduate of Georgetown University and holds a master's degree and doctorate in clinical psychology from Purdue University. She is co-author of four books: *Liars, Cheats, and Creeps: Leaving the Narcissist Behind*; *The Patient Knows: Wisdom from The Other Couch*; *Moving On From a Narcissist: How Four Women Found Happiness After Leaving Liars, Cheats, and Creeps*; and *Age Well: 8 Dimensions of Wellness as You Age*.

Dr. Martin has done research work at National Institute of Mental Health studying bi-polar disorder and at the National Institute of Child Health and Human Development studying the effects of early environment on child development. She has taught and supervised graduate and undergraduate psychology students at Purdue University, Springfield College, Bay Path University, American International College, and Westfield State University. Dr. Martin has counseled thousands of people in her 40 + years of clinical practice in New England and the Midwest. Her patient population includes children and families, individual adults, teenagers and couples.

During her career Dr. Martin has worked with thousands of women who were traumatized by domestic abuse. She facilitates therapy groups with women who are, or have been, in abusive relationships.

Dr. Martin is a guest speaker throughout the United States, presenting topics on mental health issues and relationship violence. She makes frequent appearances as a commentator on the local public television affiliate and is a guest columnist for a large metropolitan daily and its online affiliate.

Dr. Martin has been married 46 years to her husband James, and is the mother of four grown children and grandmother of eight. She lives in Western Massachusetts and New Hampshire.

Renee Forte is a pen name. She is the co-author with Dr. Patricia Martin of *Liars, Cheats, and Creeps: Leaving the Narcissist Behind* and *Moving On from a Narcissist: How Four Women Found Happiness after Leaving Liars, Cheats, and Creeps*. She chose to use a pen name to protect the identities of her wonderful children, who are innocent victims of a marriage that should never have been. The name Renee Forte translates to "Reborn Strong."

Renee is a summa cum laude graduate of college and a member of Phi Beta Kappa, with an advanced degree from a professional school and a long list of professional certifications. During her marriage, she sought therapy from Dr. Martin who said these words to her at the first appointment: "I can help. You will get through this."

Dr. Martin was right. Renee survived divorce and went on to rebuild her life with the help of Dr. Martin, The Group, and the love and support of family and friends. For Renee, sharing her experiences in this book is a way of paying it forward.

www.ingramcontent.com/pod-product-compliance
Lightning Source LLC
LaVergne TN
LVHW021236080526
838199LV00088B/4545